THREE-DIMENSIONAL
CHILDREN'S BULLETINS

THREE DIMENSIONAL CHILDREN'S BULLETINS

PATT NEWKIRK ENSING

ILLUSTRATED BY JACK BROUWER

Baker Books
A Division of Baker Book House Co
Grand Rapids, Michigan 49516

Copyright 1996 by Patt Newkirk Ensing
Illustrated by Jack Brouwer

Published by Baker Books,
a division of Baker Book House Company
P.O. Box 6287, Grand Rapids, MI 49516-6287

ISBN 0-8010-3231-8

Printed in the United States of America

CONTENTS

How often, as adults, have we enjoyed touching and poking new things to see and feel how this or that works. Children's bulletins are like that to me. Since childhood I explored with wonder the movement of things. It was fun for me to examine things and see how they were put together.

I grew up in the paper doll age. I was never satisfied with the wardrobe the books provided. I would dream and design new outfits for my special paper doll. I am still engaged in playing with paper, scissors, glue, or whatever I have around the house and I'm still having a good time. What fun it is to create!

This drive to be creative has led me to explore a new dimension in children's bulletins. It's really a new concept of presenting the Word of God. The bulletins are a clear, simple, and fun way for children to enjoy Sunday worship and learn Bible truths.

I have participated in several Children's Worship Seminars, teaching the three-dimensional bulletin session. There has been a consistent response encouraging me to put these concepts in book form.

This three-dimensional bulletin book will be like a safari through the Bible, an adventure of discovery. It will take you through some of the same "path"-ages of Scripture I have walked. You'll be re-introduced to the first and only real E. T. A stop at Wilderness Restaurant will remind us that God will provide. Were people in the Old Testament diet conscious?—A 10-day Pulse Diet Plan is included. And what about our wardrobe? . . . Peek into the Bible Closet. You'll find these and many more interesting and unusual children's bulletins, from simple ones to others that are more involved—and all are fun to do.

You may experience a twinge of delight after you have assembled a selected bulletin and you watch the results in the response of a child. I can't help but smile as I think of the joy of that moment.

I am eager to share with each of you what I have developed over the last several years. I have thoroughly enjoyed researching beyond the basic facts. To struggle with a passage that struck me or study it through the eyes of Bible scholars was a real challenge.

A little church mouse named Skeeter appeared in my children's bulletins soon after I began working on them. He's also worked his way into several pages in this book. Skeeter, a perky fellow, can do things, say things, and go places I can't. He covers for me when I misspell words. This tiny imaginary friend explains ideas and does many clever things that add interest to the bulletins. Children seem to respond immediately to his humor and the way he shares knowledge. He quickly captures their imagination and I've watched adults enjoy his capers also. You may borrow Skeeter or invent your own imaginary creature for your bulletins.

There are a lot of idea starters between these pages. Each can be adapted to other bulletins. There is no limit to the variety of combinations you can develop with a few changes.

The bulletins have been arranged by the style pattern of design. The add-ons are the easiest; I suggest them as your starting place. Each bulletin is clearly defined with procedures and a suggested list of materials and tools to use. Most also include Scripture text.

Check the resource pages for addresses for books, tracts, and other resources. A few pages are devoted to patterns and ideas for use in bulletins.

Where do children's bulletins fit in your church? Under education? evangelism? children's worship? youth? children? All children's bulletins should include some teaching. The bulletin should reach out to the children's needs.

Children should learn more about church worship, respect, and reverence in the church through the children's bulletin. There should be something each Sunday that a child or youth can identify with and think about. Encourage the children's participation by mentioning news they may know about, new family members, and other bits of information. A little humor used respectfully adds a happy note.

Children's bulletins can be used as a teaching tool, bringing forth Bible truths. Find a friend and become partners in the work of children's bulletins.

Happy Bulletin(g)!

Children's Bulletin

To decode this message below, read carefully the five-letter units. For example, this is how the directions would read:

Todec odeth ismes sageb elowr eadca reful lythe fivel etter

units

BUTJO SHUAS PARED RAHAB
THEPR OSTITU TEWIT HHERF
AMILY ANDAL LWHOB ELONG
EDTOH ERJOS HUASI XVERS
ETWEN TYFIVE

When you have decoded the message, write it on these lines:

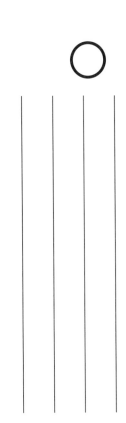

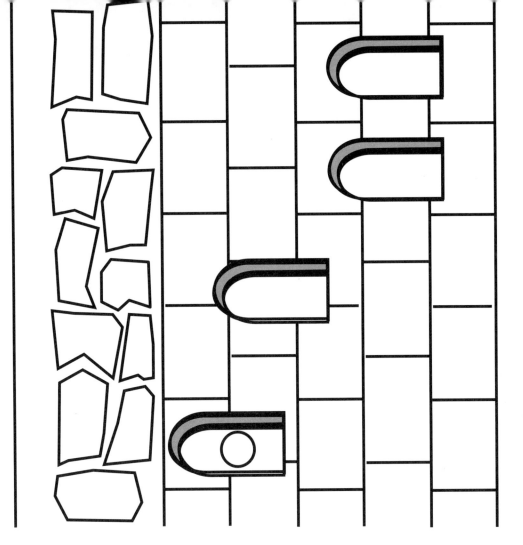

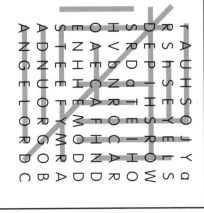

Chapter 2 of the Book of Joshua is a spy story. Read it and then list the names of three people in the story:

1. _____
2. _____
3. _____

Can you find five places mentioned in this story?

1. _____
2. _____
3. _____
4. _____
5. _____

Did you know that some of the walls around ancient cities were wide enough to have chariot races on top of them? The top of the walls were also used for traveling.

Find the hidden words in this puzzle. The letters not capitalized will spell a secret word.

```
r A U H S O J Y a
R S h S E Y E L S
D E P I H S R O W
S R D a T E I H O
H V b N R O C A R
O A E C A F H N D
E N H H E M O D D
S T E E F Y M R A
A D N U O R G O B
A N G E L O R D C
```

army	foe	Lord
commander	ground	man
earth	hand	servant
eyes	holy	shoes
face	Jericho	sword
feet	Joshua	worshiped

Secret word is the person spared in the battle of Jericho:

_____

Children's Bulletin

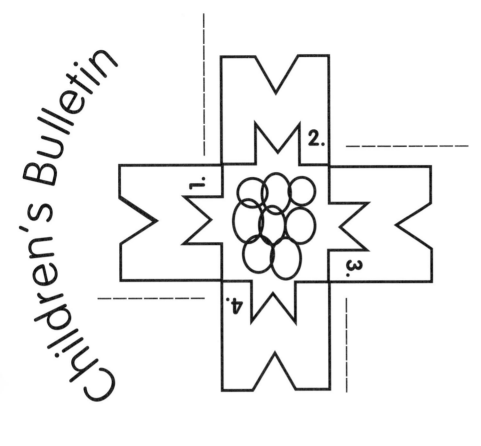

**Monuments and memorial signs that remind us to remember.
Read below and match numbers to the blanks and fill in all
the "M" words!**

1. Monuments Built to remind us to remember a special
               person or event.

2. Memorial   Something to preserve the memory of a
               person or event.

3. Memory   A person or thing to be remembered.

4. Momento   Something that serves as a reminder of
               what is past or gone.

1. _____
2. _____

**Here is an acrostic from Joshua 4:1–2,
and a portion of 3. Follow the words
in your Bible and fill in the correct
missing letters.**

The whole nation co☐pleted

the cr☐ssing

o☐

dry gro☐nd . . . .

choose twelve ☐en from

among your ☐ople

o☐e from each

☐ribe and tell them

to take up twelve ☐tones.

Today's message is all about monuments, memorials, and statues. LISTEN!

Boys and girls, remember these verses about the twelve stones? Joshua 4:6–7

v. 6 "... in the future, when your children ask you, 'What do these stones mean?'

v. 7 "... these stones are to be a memorial to the people of Israel forever."

Match these pictures to answers on these pages about monuments and memorials: signs that tell us to remember.

1. _____ A great man in history people will remember.

2. _____ Sabbath reminder of the completion of creation (Deuteronomy 5:15).

3. _____ A living memorial planted in the church yard (in memory of a loved one).

4. _____ A memorial sign from God to us that hangs in the sky after the rain (Genesis 9:13–16).

5. _____ A 12-foot cross was erected at Reed City, Michigan, home of the composer George Bennard. He wrote "The Old Rugged Cross."

6. _____ What do these stones mean? (Joshua 4:6–7)

7. _____ A memorial of peace and friendship from France.

8. _____ Egyptians built these great monuments in honor of their kings.

9. _____ A reminder that God wants us to talk to Him.

10. _____ A memorial symbol of freedom. (It rings!)

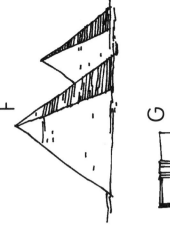

F

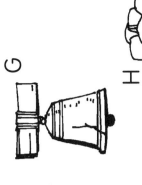

G

H

J

I

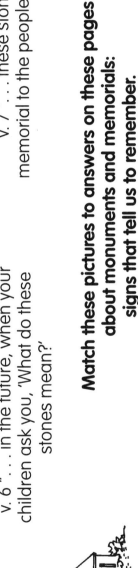

A

B

C

D

E

Children's Bulletin

Jeremiah 15:16

When your words came, I ate them; they were my joy and my heart's delight.

Life is amazing . . . babies and young children need milk. As we grow older we need solid food. Can you find the way from milk to solid food in this maze?

Children - Milk

Adults - Solid food

Eating good foods will give us strong and healthy bodies. Reading and obeying good words (God's messages) will make us strong spiritually.

We read scripture and pray to be spiritually fed. Each of the following verses has the name of a food for the body. The first letter for each food is in the box. Fill in the blanks with the remaining letters.

Jeremiah 1:11

2 Samuel 17:28

Numbers 11:5

Genesis 3:7

Numbers 11:5

Genesis 25:34

Numbers 11:5

Numbers 11:5

Deuteronomy 8:8

Exodus 16:13

John 10:7

Genesis 30:14

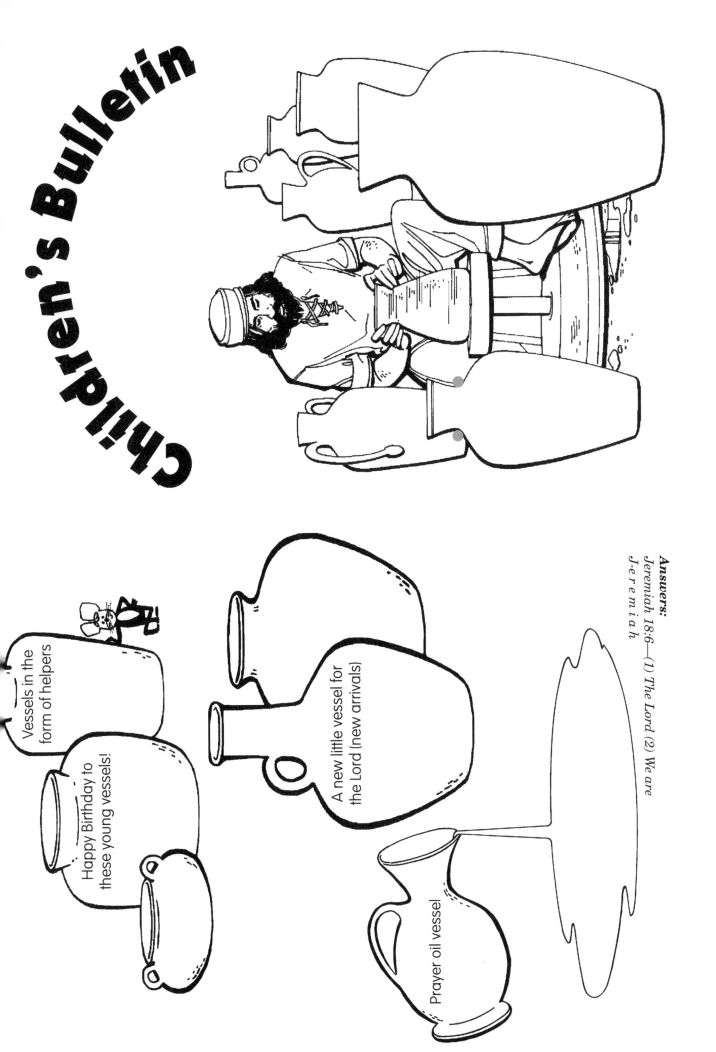

Children's Bulletin

Vessels in the form of helpers

Happy Birthday to these young vessels!

A new little vessel for the Lord (new arrivals)

Prayer oil vessel

Answers:
Jeremiah 18:6—(1) The Lord (2) We are
J-e-r-e-m-i-a h

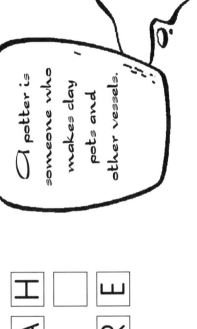

A potter is someone who makes clay pots and other vessels.

Clay is earth and water.

I	A	H	
M			
E	R	E	

Solve the square connection puzzle. Figure out which letter belongs in the empty square. When you find it, start with that letter and go around all squares to discover the book of the Bible that today's passage is from. (Clue: it is the tenth letter in the alphabet.)

_____ 18:1–12

Read Jeremiah 18:6.

1. Who is the potter? _____

2. Who is the clay? _____

Do you see different shapes of pottery and vases? Skeeter, with the help of a pencil bigger than he is, drew a face on one. Put faces on the others. You can draw arms and legs, too. Have fun. Today's message reminds us God can mold us, just as the potter molds the clay!

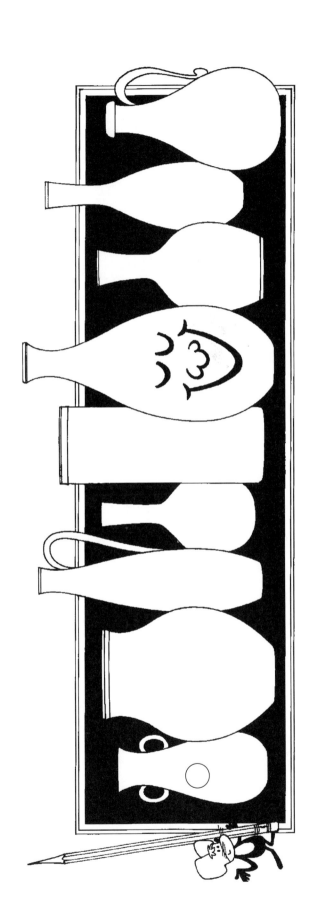

What do you remember most about Daniel?
Can you remember which events were first
and which events followed in Daniel's life? See
if you can put the following in the correct order.
Number them 1 through 6.

_____ A. Interpreted dreams

_____ B. Handwriting on the wall

_____ C. Taken captive

_____ D. Lion's den

_____ E. Obeyed God

_____ F. Fiery furnace

_____ G. Daniel's special diet

Draw a picture of your favorite foods.

"Pulse Plan"
Glue
box
here

Answers:
(1) Daniel (2) Eunuch (3) meat (4) drink (5) kings
(1) E, (2) C, (3) G, (4) A, (5) F, (6) B, (7) D

Look at these fun figures and find letters. Fill the blanks with the letters. Each is the name of a person or thing in Daniel's story.

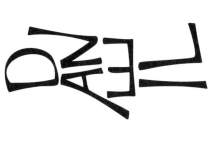

1. _____

2. _____

3. _____

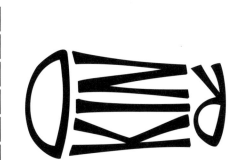

4. _____

5. _____

What is "pulse"?

_____

_____

Find the answers in Daniel 1:

1. How many days?

   verse 15: at the end of _____ days they looked healthier.

2. What did God give Daniel and his three friends?

   verse 17: God gave them _____ and _____

   _____ of all kinds of _____ and

   _____

They obeyed the laws of God, given to Moses.

PREPARING MEAT CORRECTLY		Babylon	Hebrew
EATING HABITS OF BABYLON			
DANIEL'S DAILY PULSE PLAN			
FOOD "FIT" FOR THE KING		God	
TO EAT OR NOT TO EAT		Neb	
THE EUNUCH'S GUIDELINES FOR CAPTIVES		Melzar	
TO EAT OR NOT TO EAT	Daniel		

Children's Bulletin

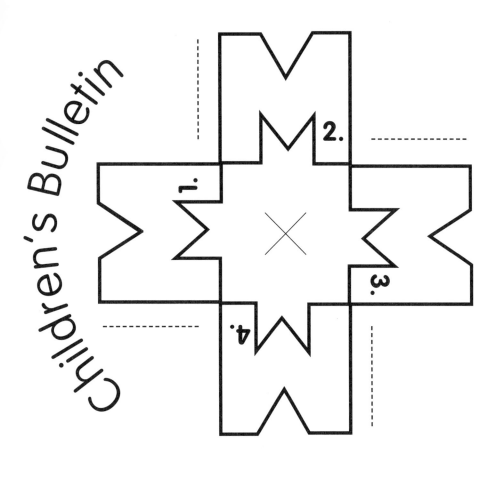

1.
2.
3.
4.

M&Ms emphasize Micah the Minor prophet.

Using the capital "M" in the logo above fill in the matching numbers with these words.

Facts: (1.) **Micah** was a (2.) **Minor** prophet. He was a native of (3.) **Moresheth** with a (4.) **Message** from God to all people.

Famous Bible Mountains

Several mountains are mentioned in the Bible. Noah's ark finally stopped on Mount Ararat. Can you remember the names of other mountains talked about in the Bible? Do you remember what happened on these mountains?

(1.) Mountain where Solomon's temple was built.

(2.) God gave Moses the Ten Commandments on this mountain.

(3.) Jesus prayed on this mountain, and he also went to heaven from this mountain.

(4.) Jesus taught on this mountain. One of the things he said was, "Blessed are the meek."

(5.) Jesus was transfigured on this mountain. It is also the place where Deborah and Gideon faced their enemies.

Now have some fun with letters that look like mountains and valleys. Start with drawing the letter M, then W. You think of other letters.

Follow each path through the letters. Fill the letters in the blanks for a message. Join the dots to find something we all can have.

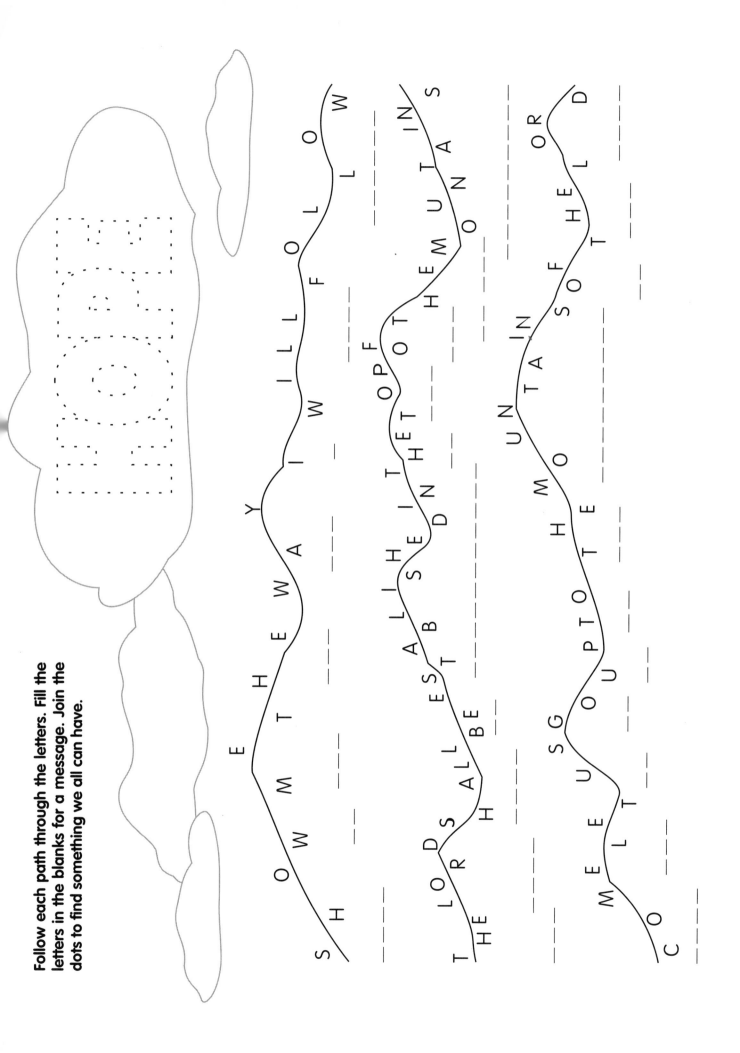

Children's Bulletin

Color or shade all the squares with even numbers (2, 4, 6, 8) to discover a very important word.

2	8	5	3	4	1	6	2	4	8
8	2	7	1	2	3	4	5	9	4
6	4	3	9	6	7	6	9	3	2
4	3	8	1	6	1	8	3	3	6
2	5	6	7	8	9	2	3	5	8
2	3	5	6	4	3	4	7	9	4
6	9	7	4	2	3	2	5	1	6
8	1	5	8	6	7	6	8	4	2

I like these words from Titus 2:12 (also even numbers!):

"It teaches us to say **'NO'** to ungodliness and worldly passions." (NIV) **JUST SAY NO** to temptation!

Draw a picture of how you can **JUST SAY NO** to temptation.

Temptation: Someone may try to talk us into doing something we should not do. It is the wrong choice to let temptation take over and lead us to say or do something we will be sorry for.

Jesus was prepared to face temptation. Yes, he was the Son of God. But he also was filled with the Word of God, and the Holy Spirit was with him. He was able to stand against Satan.

Count all the T's in today's bulletin. How many can you find? _____

"Away from me, Satan!" Matthew 4:10
"Do not put the Lord your God to the test." Luke 4:12

Luke's scribe forgo___ all ___he T's. Can you pu___ ___hem in for Luke? This is based on Luke 4:

Dear boys and girls,

Wi__h pen in hand, I am wri___ing ___he accoun___ of how ___he ministry of Jesus began. Jesus had been in ___he wilderness abou__ for___y days. He had no__ ea__en during ___ha__ ___ime. He was alone and hungry. ___he devil came ___o Jesus and ___aun___ed him by saying, "Jus___ __urn __his s__one in__o bread." Jesus was no___ ___emp___ed. Jesus said, "I__ is wri___en, ___ha___ man shall no__ live on bread alone" (v. 4).

___hen ___he devil ___ook Jesus ___o ___he moun___ain ___op. ___he devil said ___o Jesus,
"See all ___his. I will give i___ ___o you if you worship only me."
Jesus said, i___ is wri___en, worship ___he Lord your God and serve him only" (v.8).

___he devil wasn'___ happy. ___hen he ___ook Jesus ___o ___he highes___ poin___ of ___he ___emple and said, "If you are ___he Son of God, throw yourself down from here."

Again Jesus spoke ___o ___he devil and said, "Do no___ put___ ___he Lord your God ___o ___he ___es___" (v. 12).

I, Luke, ___he physician, dear friend and follower of Jesus, wri__e ___hese words ___o remind you!

Don'___ le___ ___he devil ___emp___ you by ___elling lies ___o you. ___he devil will ___ry ___o ge___ you ___o do some___hing you don'___ wan___ ___o do. ___ha___'s ___he ___ime ___o pray ___o Jesus and ask him ___o help you. First John 4:4 will also remind you: "___he one who is in you is grea___er ___han ___he one who is in ___he world."

CHILDREN'S BULLETIN

GREATEST FISH STORY

Would you like to make a paper fish net? Fold a small piece of paper like you do to make a fan. With a scissors, make cuts about a half inch apart almost to the opposite side along the edge of one side. Do the same along the opposite side, making cuts in between your first cuts. Open carefully. Hold by the ends and pull to stretch the paper. Once you learn how to make a small net, you can make them larger. Isn't this fun?

Skeeter and his friend looked for more information about fish. They discovered that the Greek language (what the New Testament was written in) has over 400 names for fish. That's no fish story.

Fish that had fins and scales were accepted as clean food for the Hebrews to eat. Any other fish were unclean.

fold

pull and stretch

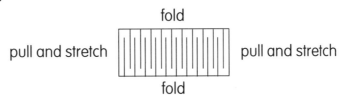

pull and stretch

fold

Answers to Skip a Letter:

"They forsook all and followed him."

Locate verse:
Luke 5:11 (KJV)

Fishes with wishes:
Our anchor holds. Please remember:

Greatest Fish Story answers:
1. They caught a large number of fish.
2. Jesus
3. The people and Simon Peter
4. Simon Peter
5. Jesus
6. James, John, and Simon Peter

A message is in the deep waters. Start with the letter T and go up and around, skipping every other letter. Write the letters you land on in the blanks.

__ __ __ __   __ __ __ __ __   __ __ __

__ __ __   __ __ __ __ __   __ __ __

__ __ __

CAN YOU LOCATE THIS VERSE IN YOUR BIBLE?

Book:

Chapter:

Verse:

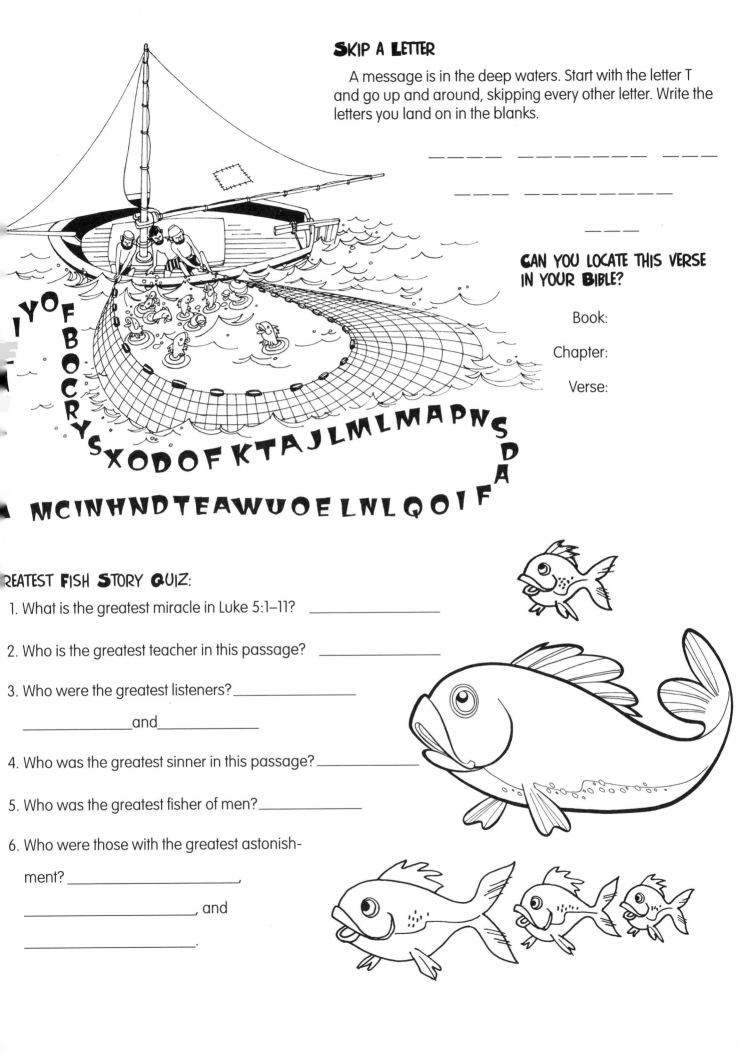

I Y O F B O C R Y S X O D O F K T A J L M L M A P N S D A

A M C I N H N D T E A W U O E L N L Q O I F

GREATEST FISH STORY QUIZ:

1. What is the greatest miracle in Luke 5:1–11? _____

2. Who is the greatest teacher in this passage? _____

3. Who were the greatest listeners?_____

   _____and_____

4. Who was the greatest sinner in this passage?_____

5. Who was the greatest fisher of men?_____

6. Who were those with the greatest astonish-

   ment? _____,

   _____, and

   _____.

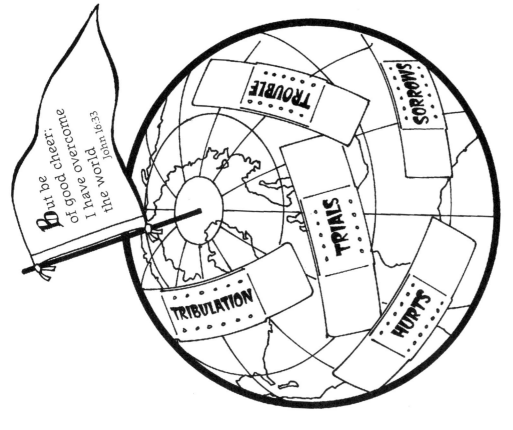

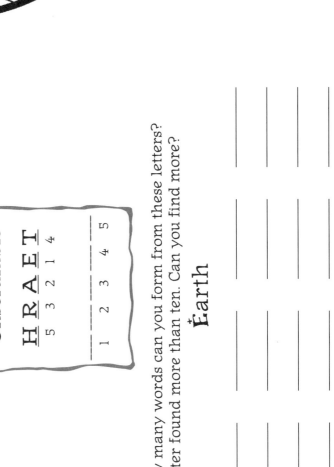

But be
of good cheer:
I have overcome
the world.
John 16:33

The earth was a gift to us.

Genesis 1:10:

God called the _____ " _____ " . . . . And
God saw that it was good.

Numbers 14:21:

The glory of the Lord fills the whole _____ .

1 Corinthians 10:26:

The _____ is the Lord's, and everything in it.

Unscramble

H   R   A   E   T
5   3   2   1   4

__ __ __ __ __
1   2   3   4   5

How many words can you form from these letters?
Skeeter found more than ten. Can you find more?

Earth

_____ _____ _____

_____ _____ _____

_____ _____ _____

When you are feeling very sad read John 16:16–33.

1. We can pray (1 Thessalonians 5:17)
2. We can claim (1 John 4:4)
3. When we get older (Ephesians 4:13)
4. We can learn (Philippians 4:6)
5. We can find (Philippians 4:7)
6. We can think about (Philippians 4:8)

Glue Here

and then after a little while you will see me.

John 16:16

On the bulletin this Sunday is a world covered with Band-aids. are handy for &  They may make your hurts feel better.

The is full of hurts, sorrows, & trials. can't cover them.

know some 1 who heal a hurt better also know some- thing that help us better than a .

than any 1 else know.

That some 1 is Jesus.

That something is the Bible.

We pray & ask Jesus for strength & courage.

We read God's Word.

That will help us 2 wise.

Children's Bulletin

He Wanted His Own Way

Once a trap was baited with a dainty piece of cheese.
It tickled so a little mouse it almost made him sneeze.
An old mouse said,
"There's danger . . . be careful where you go."
"I don't care,"
said Mousie, "I don't think you know."
So he walked in boldly. Nobody was in sight.
First he took a nibble,
then he took a bite.
The trap closed together, SNAP!
And there Mousie lay,
caught tight within the trap,
'cause he wanted his own way.

. . . That is why God let go of them and let them do all these
evil things.

I WANT TO DO THIS ONE THING.

Romans 1:26 (TLB)

The sea of disobedience leads to the deep, deep, deep water of many sins.

Color what God says yellow.
Color what Skeeter says blue.

Children's Bulletin

... to live in

Harmony

... with one voice

GLORIFY GOD

Romans 15:5,6

Praising _____ and enjoying the favor of all the _____. And the Lord (+) _____ 2 their number daily those who were _____ saved.
Acts 2:47

DO ALL THE GOOD YOU CAN,
BY ALL THE MEANS YOU CAN,
IN ALL THE WAYS YOU CAN,
IN ALL THE PLACES YOU CAN,
AT ALL THE TIMES YOU CAN,
TO ALL THE PEOPLE YOU CAN,
AS LONG AS YOU EVER CAN.
JOHN WESLEY

If God is taken out of Good,

nothing

(o)

is left!

Answers

```
G O O D   G I F T S  J
T H E   O S W E N  U
D R A E Y B H A B S
R E E H C R I O S T
E B C E S I O Z  A
H O B K R K U R D N
P H E A R T S O R D
E Y M T R O F M O C
H A A N S I W A L  T
S V N W O R D S A W
```

GLORIFY GOD

Some Bible verses have the word good in them, like Matthew 5:16:

Let your light shine before men, that they may see your good deeds and praise your Father in heaven.

Here is a word search of some "good" works. Some of them are from the Bible. Find the words in capitals.
(Word search):

```
G O O D G I F T S J
T H E E O S W E N U
D R A E Y B H A B S
R E E H C R T O S T
E B C E S I O Z I A
H O B K R K U R D N
P H E A R T S O R D
E Y M T R O F M O C
H A A N S I W A L T
S V N W O R D S A W
```

GOODBYE

GOOD BOOK

GOOD CHEER (John 16:33 KJV)

GOOD COMFORT (Matthew 9:22 KJV)

GOOD GIFT (James 1:17)

GOOD

GOOD HEART

JUST AND GOOD (Romans 7:12 KJV)

LAW IS GOOD (1 Timothy 1:8)

LORD IS GOOD (Psalm 34:8)

GOOD MAN (Psalm 37:23 KJV)

GOOD NAME (Proverbs 22:1)

GOOD NEWS (Proverbs 25:25)

GOOD SAMARITAN (Story of: Luke 10:30–37)

GOOD SHEPHERD (John 10:11)

TAKE GOOD HEED (John 23:11)

THEE GOOD (Genesis 32:12 KJV)

GOOD TO US (1 Samuel 25:15)

WAS GOOD (Genesis 1:4)

GOOD WAY (Jeremiah 6:16)

YEAR WITH THY GOODNESS (Psalm 65:11 KJV)

GOOD WORD (Proverbs 12:25 KJV)

I Corinthians 2:9

__t __s written:

"No 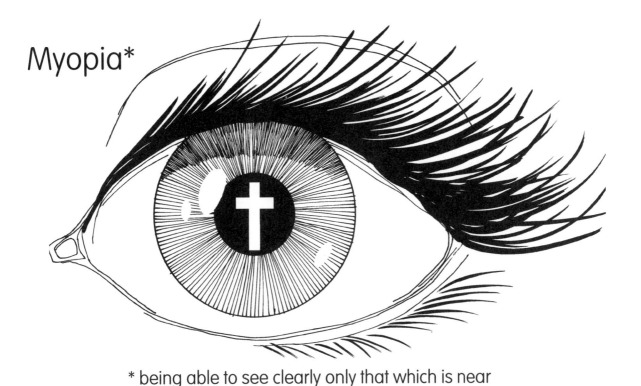 has seen, no 👂 has heard, no m__nd has conce__ved what God has prepared 4 those who ♡ h__m."

Children's Bulletin

Myopia*

* being able to see clearly only that which is near

- Cover your left eye and read line 1.
- Cover your right eye and read line 2.
- Cover your left eye and read line 3.
- Cover your right eye and read line 4.
- With both eyes read line 5.

Best vision is 20/20

"KEEP YOUR EYES ON CHRIST"

Children's Bulletin

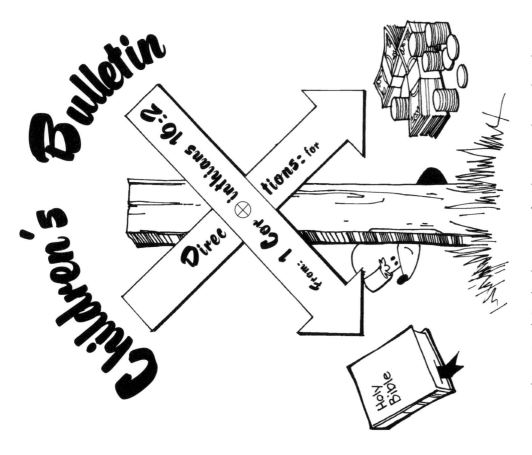

Direc⊗tions: for
from: 1 Corinthians 16:2

Holy Bible

Paul received God's directions for the Corinthian church and for our church today.

On the first day of every week, each one of you should set aside a sum of money in keeping with your income.

1 Corinthians 16:2:

Counting Cash and Other Things
by Skeeter

Counting began thousands of years ago.

One counts to get the total amount.

Noah counted the animals two by two in the ark.

Some people count sheep when they can't sleep.

Some people are anxious about tomorrow and they count their chickens before they hatch! (People are so funny.)

My Uncle Mousker told me that in England there were counting houses (I guess like bookkeeping offices).

In Europe, there are noblemen who are called counts. And a noblewoman is called a countess.

The world is big and has a lot of countries.

Families can walk or take a ride to the countryside.

Law is practiced at the County Court House to protect people from counterfeiters. People will be held accountable for their deeds.

The people I live with are Christians and they count their blessings.

Miss Mousette, my Sunday School teacher, told us Moses had a glowing countenance after he spoke with God.

Now that is a lot of counts to be accountable for.

Underline each word that has count in it and count them all. How many have you counted? _____

Do you earn an allowance? YES or NO
(circle your answer)

How much do you earn? _____

Do you earn your money by helping mom and dad? YES or NO
(circle your answer)

This is a division sign in math. ÷

Divide what you earn by 10 and see what answer you get.

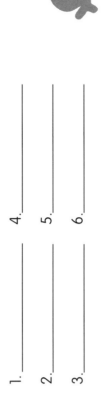

$$10\,\overline{)}$$

_____ (your tithe)
_____ (what you earn)

Can you think of some other words for money? List six that start with the letter C.

1. _____   4. _____

2. _____   5. _____

3. _____   6. _____

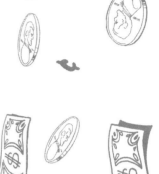

Skeeter, Skeeter sitting on the fence
trying to make a dollar out of 15¢

The "Change" Ladder

Change only one letter in each word as you move down to the next word.

Start with the word CASH. End with the word DIME.

_____ Money

_____ Something to carry things in

_____ A way people feel about others

_____ Money paid for a bus ride

_____ To become well known

_____ Nursery rhyme, "One for my master and one for my . . . "

_____ One tenth of a dollar

Children's Bulletin

We don't know the names of the persons who wrote the Apostles' Creed. When the church was very young, people used the creed as a way to remember what the apostles taught and what Christians believe.

Look up these verses in your Bible to help you understand the creed. Fill in the blanks with some similar words you find in your Bible.

1. Blessed be Abram by _____ of _____ and _____ , _____ . *Genesis 14:19*

2. And a voice came from heaven: "You are my _____ whom I love . . ." *Mark 1:11*

3. The _____ will be with child and give birth to a son. *Matthew 1:23*

4. Pilate handed him over to them to be _____ . *JOHN 19:16*

5. We believe that Jesus _____ and _____ again. *1 Thessalonians 4:14*

6. With great power the apostles continued to testify to the _____ of the Lord Jesus. *Acts 4:33*

Answers:

Stack-a-Word—
1. Creator   2. father
3. heaven   4. almighty
5. God   6. believe
7. earth

Fill-in-blanks—
1. God Most High (Almighty)
   creator, heaven, earth
2. Son   3. virgin
4. crucified   5. died, rose
6. resurrection

Apostles' Creed Stack-a-Word

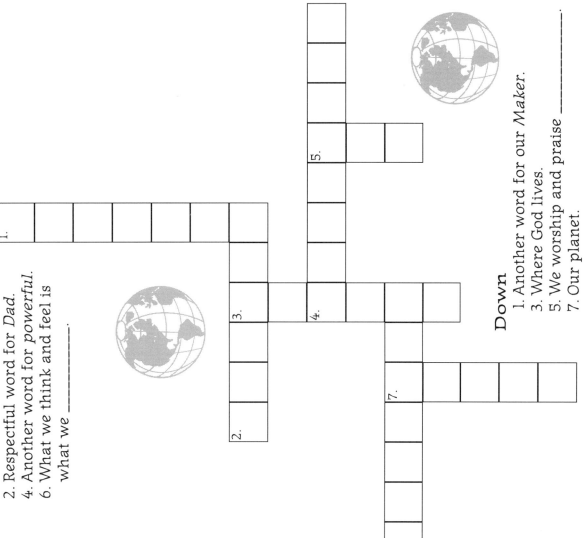

Across

2. Respectful word for *Dad.*
4. Another word for *powerful.*
6. What we think and feel is what we _____.

Down

1. Another word for our *Maker.*
3. Where God lives.
5. We worship and praise _____.
7. Our planet.

Apostles' Creed

I believe in God, the Father almighty, Creator of heaven and earth. I believe in Jesus Christ, his only Son, our Lord, who was conceived by the Holy Spirit and born of the virgin Mary. He suffered under Pontius Pilate, was crucified, died, and was buried; he descended to Hell. The third day he rose again from the dead. He ascended to Heaven and is seated at the right hand of God the Father almighty. From there he will come to judge the living and the dead. I believe in the Holy Spirit, the holy catholic church, the communion of saints, the forgiveness of sins, the resurrection of the body, and the life everlasting. Amen.

Radiant Church

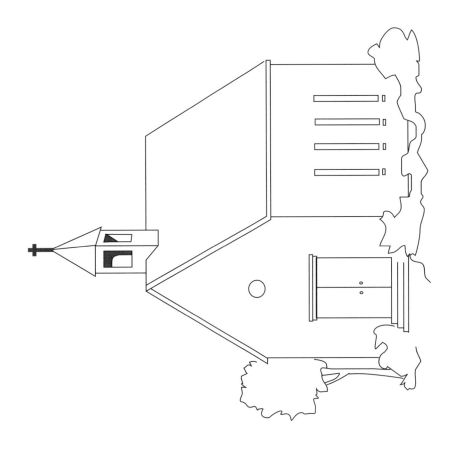

" . . . a radiant church, without stain or wrinkle or any other blem-
ish, but holy and blameless."

Ephesians 5:27

Can you draw one continuous line to form a church building
like the one drawn below, without lifting your pencil from the
paper and without drawing over the same line twice? (You may
lift your pencil to draw a cross on the peak of the church.)

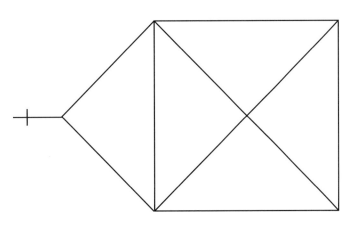

X marks the spot where we should be each Sunday!

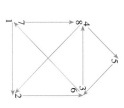

Answers:

(1) T   (2) F   (3) F   (4) F   (5) F   (6) T
(7) T   (8) T   (9) F   (10) F (11) T (12) T
(13) F (14) T (15) T (16) T

The "radiant church" spoken of in Ephesians 5:1–33 has guidelines to follow. Circle the letter under T if the guideline is true. Circle the letter under F if the guideline is false. Then put the letters you circled into the boxes with matching numbers below.

		T	F
1.	Paul wrote to the Ephesian church.	H	A
2.	The Ephesian church was the only church with problems.	E	O
3.	Paul's message was only for church leaders.	J	L
4.	Don't walk in love.	O	Y
5.	But you don't have to love everyone.	A	A
6.	Don't covet.	N	I
7.	No foolish talking or jesting.	D	S
8.	Don't associate with bad people.	B	C

		T	F
9.	There are no bad people in the world.	B	L
10.	You can have idols.	G	A
11.	Love Christ with all your heart.	M	P
12	Walk uprightly.	E	A
13.	You can grumble all you want.	I	L
14.	Sing psalms and hymns of praise.	E	O
15.	You can be happy.	S	T
16.	We are all members together.	S	E

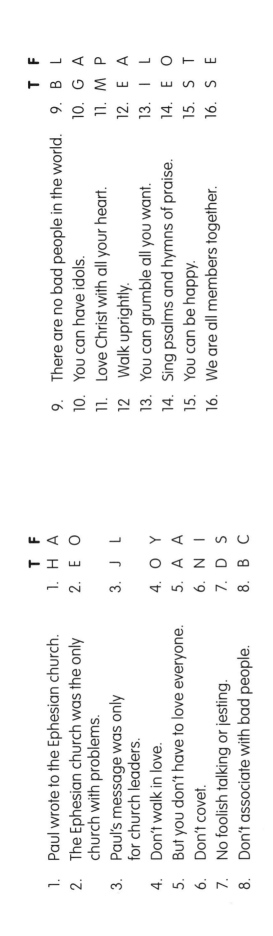
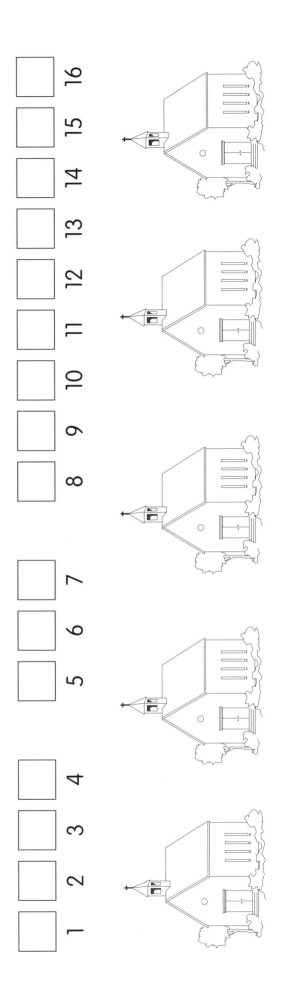

1	2	3	4	5	6	7	8	9	10	11	12	13	14	15	16
□	□	□	□	□	□	□	□	□	□	□	□	□	□	□	□

Children's Bulletin

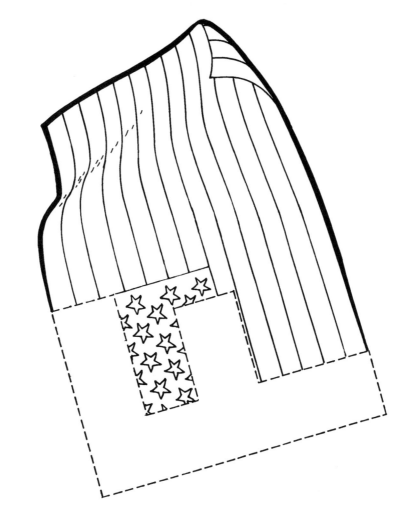

Skeeter is busy counting all the F's in today's bulletin. How many are there? _____

Fun on the fourth with pop can tabs! Trace around one; what can you see? Use your imagination to draw a critter.

Find the five puzzle pieces in the corner bookmark pocket. Arrange them to form the letter F in the U.S. flag.

Think about words starting with F that tell about July 4th.

1. Enjoyment _____

2. Piece of cloth _____

3. Special day _____

4. Liberty _____

5. Celebration _____

6. Pals or chums _____

7. Small explosives _____

Draw a picture here of your answers to # 2 and # 7.

July Fourth is our nation's birthday.

Teacher: "Who wrote, 'Oh, Say Can You See?'"
Student: "An eye doctor."

Four Freedoms. Fill in the blanks with freedom words. Ask your parents to help with this.

1. Freedom of _____

2. Freedom of _____

3. Freedom from _____

4. Freedom from _____

Children's Bulletin

They will walk with me, dressed in white, for 'they are worthy.'
Revelation 3:4

An acrostic from Revelation 3:1–3.

re ☐ ains	v. 2
ang ☐ l	v. 1
☐ even spirits	v. 1
seven ☐ tars	v. 1
w ☐ ke up	v. 2
stren ☐ then	v. 2
rem ☐ mber	v. 3

Acrostic—message

How many word can you make from the letters in BOOK OF LIFE?

Look for the letters in each line. Starting with 'H' in first line, go from left to right line by line. Fill in blanks below as you do.

```
2 H 3 3 E 6 5 7 W 5 H 4 O 3
O 4 V E 3 R C 6 O 2 8 M E 9
9 S 2 W I 4 L 8 7 L 4 3 5 5
L 6 I K 4 E 3 T 5 H 2 E M, 6
2 B 7 2 E 8 D 6 R E 4 5 7 S
S E 4 D 7 1 5 N 8 W 3 H 8 8
3 I T 3 E. 6 1 3 W 5 I 4 L L
N 5 E 7 V 4 E R 8 B 4 L 6 2
6 O 6 T 2 O 8 U T 5 H 3 I S
N 7 A 5 M E 3 F 7 R 7 O M 4
8 T 2 H 6 E 3 7 B 4 O O 6 K
O 2 F 5 L 4 1 4 F 6 8 5 E. 8
```

_ _ _   _ _ _

_ _ _ _ _ _ _ _ _   _ _ _ _   _ _ _ _ _   _ _   _ _ _ _ _ _ _ '   _ _ _ _ _ _ _

_ _ _ _ _ _ ,   _ _ _   _   _ _ _ _   _ _ _ _ _   _ _ _ _

_ _ _   _ _ _ _   _ _ _ _   _ _ _   _ _ _ _ .

REVELATION 3:5

Write your name and the names of your parents, brothers, sisters, cousins, grand-parents, and friends here:

_____

_____

_____

_____

_____

_____

_____

_____

_____

_____

Book of Life — Vol. 5
Book of Life — Vol. 6
Book of Life — Vol. 7
Book of Life — Vol. 8
Book of Life — Vol. 9
Book of Life — Vol. 10
Book of Life — Vol. 11
Book of Life — Vol. 12
Book of Life — Vol. 13
Book of Life — Vol. 14
Book of Life — Vol. 15
Book of Life — Vol. 16
Book of Life — Vol. 17

Vol. 1 — Book of Life
Vol. 2 — Book of Life
Vol. 3 — Book of Life
Vol. 4 — Book of Life

Children's Bulletin

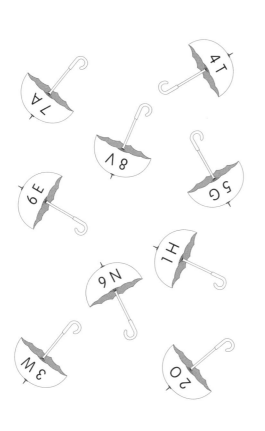

Put the letters in the numbered umbrellas into the matching numbered blanks below to find a hidden message.

7 A   4 T

8 V   5 G

6 E

9 N   1 H

3 W   2 O

$\overline{1}\ \overline{2}\ \overline{3}$ $\overline{4}\ \overline{2}$ $\overline{5}\ \overline{6}\ \overline{4}$

$\overline{4}\ \overline{2}$ $\overline{1}\ \overline{6}\ \overline{7}\ \overline{8}\ \overline{6}\ \overline{9}$

Fill in the missing letter o's.

F_r G_d s_ l_ved the w_rld   that

he gave his __ne and __nly s__n.

John 3:16

Help Skeeter match each section of his umbrella with one of the colors listed above. (Hint: Read the paragraph about colors on the opposite page first)

A. Gold   C. Green
B. White   D. Red
              E. Black

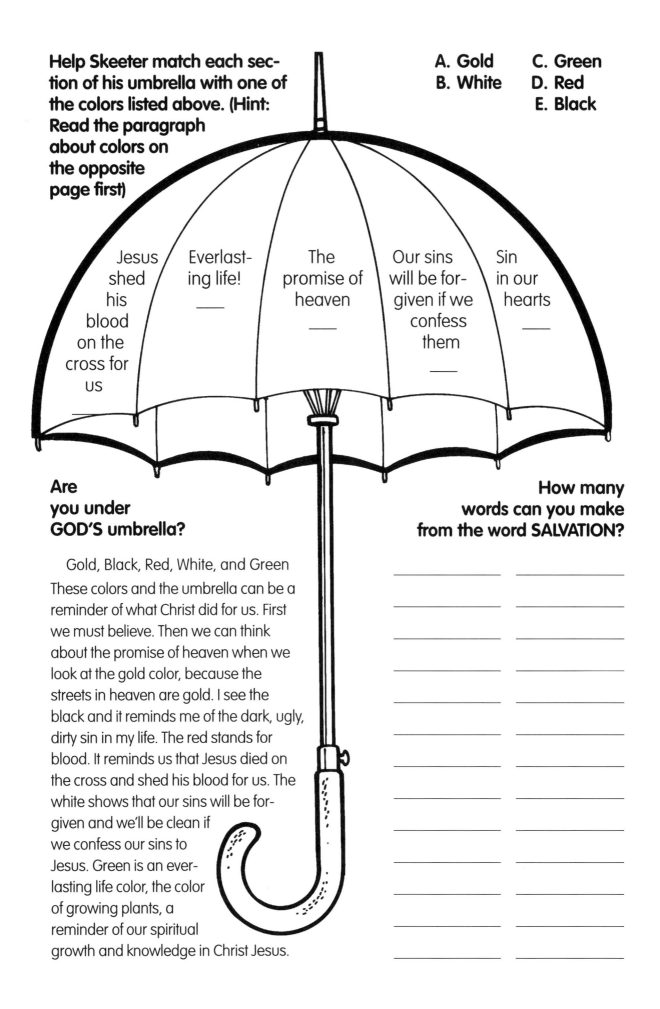

Jesus shed his blood on the cross for us ___

Everlasting life! ___

The promise of heaven ___

Our sins will be forgiven if we confess them ___

Sin in our hearts ___

Are you under GOD'S umbrella?

Gold, Black, Red, White, and Green These colors and the umbrella can be a reminder of what Christ did for us. First we must believe. Then we can think about the promise of heaven when we look at the gold color, because the streets in heaven are gold. I see the black and it reminds me of the dark, ugly, dirty sin in my life. The red stands for blood. It reminds us that Jesus died on the cross and shed his blood for us. The white shows that our sins will be forgiven and we'll be clean if we confess our sins to Jesus. Green is an everlasting life color, the color of growing plants, a reminder of our spiritual growth and knowledge in Christ Jesus.

How many words can you make from the word SALVATION?

_____ _____
_____ _____
_____ _____
_____ _____
_____ _____
_____ _____
_____ _____
_____ _____
_____ _____
_____ _____
_____ _____
_____ _____

Mission Word Find

You can find a verse hidden in the word find. Read each line left to right and write the lowercase letters you find in the blanks below. Look up the verse in your Bible.

Bible	help	open doors
Billy Graham	"Here am I, send	our prayer
Care	me."	out reach
climate	home	praise
culture	J. Hudson Taylor	safety
David Livingstone	J. Elliot	study
faith	Jesus	teach
family life	Love for others	"Whom shall I send?"
fruitfulness	Lord	William Carey
God	medical	witness
grow in grace	needs	

```
J M A M A H A R G Y L L I B D
E t F R U I T F U L N E S S A
S H O U T S G R O W T H h e V
U C E g E R M E D I C A L D I
S L r R J E C A R G e a N t D
Y I B L E Y H C O S N E P O L
E M W E R A O H L c S o m m I
R A I F U R M F A I T H T S V
A T T I T P E I L S R O O D I
C E N L L L i L S H s s I E N
M S E Y U E A i o E C n L E G
A I S L C H m a S S N A L N S
L A S I S A F E T Y E D E t T
L R L M t h e U C R w 2 M T O
L P O A G O D 8 R 1 9 & J E N
I H 2 F O Y S U R I B I B L E
W J H U D S O N T A Y L O R D
```

____ ____ ____ ____ ____ ____ ____

____ ____ ____ ____ ____ : ____

Day Three
Tuesday

God will bless the missionaries' families, those with young children and those who have chilren away at school.

Day Five
Thursday

God will be with missionaries as they try to tell people about the love of Jesus. Ask God to give them the right words to say.

Day Two
Monday

God will keep missionaries healthy, and happy, and safe from things that could hurt them.

Day
Seven
Saturday

God will help missionaries to work with the tribes and government of the country. Pray that God will make it possible for missionaries to witnessto such rulers.

Day Four
Wednesday

God will help the missionaries to learn and speak the language and get used to living in a strange country.

Day One
Sunday

God will help missionaries to be strong Christians, growing stronger every day.

Day Six
Friday

God will help missionaries to get along with other people who help them tell the good news about Jesus.

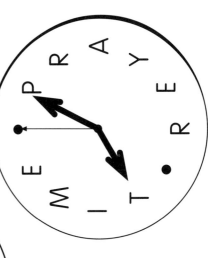

M E P R A Y I T R E

Skeeter ran across the keyboard of the computer and misspelled all the towns on Paul's journey. Can you unscramble the letters and match each word to those above? Be sure to put the number in the blanks.

Example: #12 ETRY is Tyre.

___Syria   ___Antioch   ___Philippi   ___Tyre

___Corinth   ___Caesarea   ___Greece   ___Athens

___Galatia   ___Macedonia   ___Lystra   ___Malta

___Ephesus   ___Jerusalem   ___Thessalonica

1. CHIANTO
2. TYSLAR
3. AATAILG
4. INAMEADOC
5. HIPPILIP
6. LINESASHCOAT
7. SENATH
8. COTRNIH
9. SEESUPH
10. RACESAIA
11. USAEJERLM
12. ETRY
13. RISAY
14. ATALM
15. ERGECE

Epistle* Word Find

```
E G A L A T I A N S
S E L T S I P E T N
N P H I L E M O N A
A N C O R I N T H I A N S
I A M E A J A M E S E O I
S N A I N O L A S S E H T
E I P E T S N A M O R S I
H E B R E W S E I L I E T
P D R E T E P N H O J O U
E U T I M O T H Y C A E S
I J S N A I P P I L I H P
```

* epistles are letters

Find the sixteen names on the mailbox hidden in this puzzle

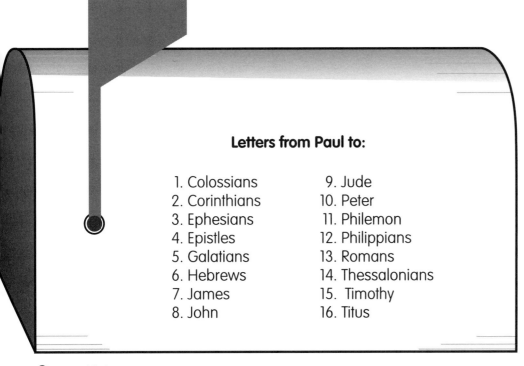

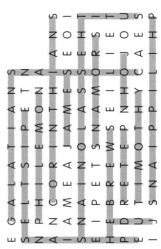

Letters from Paul to:

1. Colossians
2. Corinthians
3. Ephesians
4. Epistles
5. Galatians
6. Hebrews
7. James
8. John
9. Jude
10. Peter
11. Philemon
12. Philippians
13. Romans
14. Thessalonians
15. Timothy
16. Titus

Note:
Numbers 7, 8, 9, and 10 were not written by Paul

Fancy letters

Unscramble the letters in these drawings to find the names to four Christmas things.

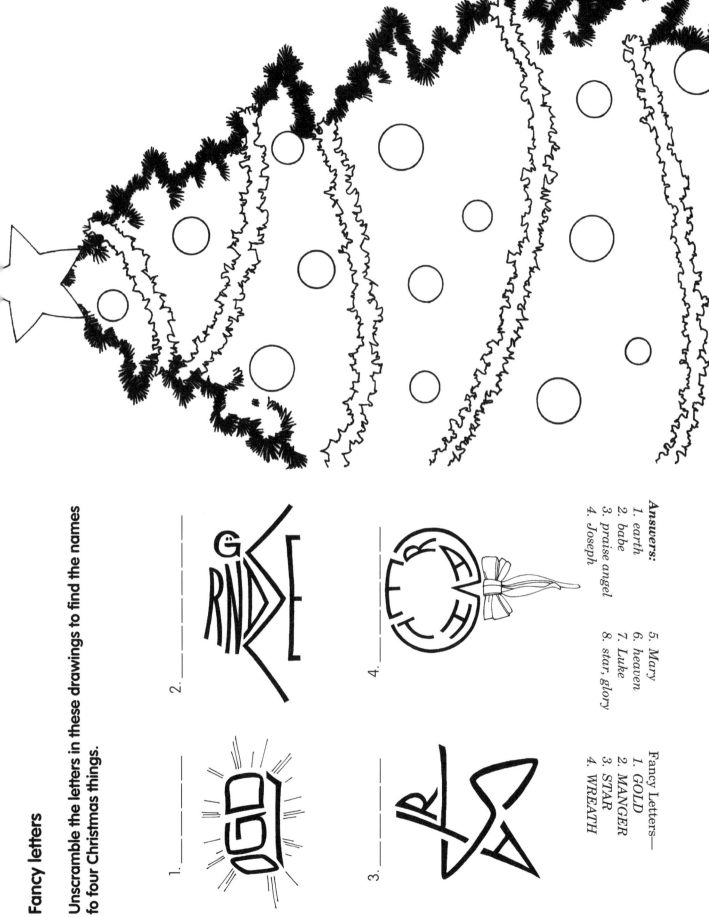

1. ___

2. ___

3. ___

4. ___

Several words from Luke 2

Several words from Luke 2 words are spread between words in these sentences. (There may be more than one Luke 2 word in each sentence.) Circle the words when you find them.

This one is done for you:
Search for the word <u>scan</u>.
Boys and <u>girls can learn</u> and have fun.

angel   earth   star   heaven   Joseph
Luke   praise   babe   glory   Mary

1. Children listen well with each ear. The message today is for everyone.
2. A little lamb softly says, "Ba." "Be still," says its mother.
3. The herdsman took his harp, raised it upon his knee and plucked the strings quietly while Eve sang elegantly.
4. Jose, physician of the small village, is a well respected man.
5. Be careful, don't mar your bike!
6. Heave, now, and move the heavy boulder.
7. Wear your mukluk, Eric.
8. Les, target of ridicule, tramped along singing, "Lo, rye grass in the distance I see."

Today in the town of David a Savior has been born to you; he is Christ the Lord.

Luke 2:11

Stack-A-Word

Now use the words you found in each sentence as clues for the following stack-a-word. Fill in the words putting the first letter in the numbered box that matches the sentence number.

Children's Bulletin

Wilderness RESTAURANT

God provided food daily for the people of Israel.

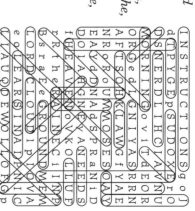

Letter Link—Find as many words as you can in this series of letters. Skeeter found 30. Can you find more?

QUAILAWILDERNESSINAISRAELISTENEEDSINN
EDESERTESTHEVENINGRUMBLINGGODAILYEARAIN

_____

_____

_____

_____

_____

_____

_____

_____

_____

_____

Wilderness Word Find:

In the message from Exodus 16:1–15, you will find many of these words. There is a hidden message, too: In the blanks, write down the letters that are not capitalized, starting with the top line and always starting over at the left side of the next line and going across to the right side.

```
I N S T R U C T I O N S g o J
d T P Y G E p S U D O X E r O
D S N E R D L I H C I A V N U
M O R N I N G o v i T d E O R
O R G e d L G N I Y A S R R N
A F T S O H K L A W G f Y A E
N R o U M M O S E S O A Y
E A Y d D N A d S P R a N i D
D O I A H G N E Y A N E E D S
f H E A V E N o V K O L L U F
r R t h e R A I N E C i I N P
B s a E e G R O U N D M E M
L O R D C L O U D I P I O V A
e o L E A R S I N A I P N I C
L I A U Q D E W O L L O F G p
W l e M U R M U R E D A I L Y
```

Aaron	glory	needs	wilderness
bread	rain	people	spake
camp	ground	quail	walk
children	heard		
cloud	heaven	Sinai	
daily	hoarfrost	saying	
day	host	sin	
dew	hunger		
eat	instructions		
Egypt	Israel		
Elim	journey		
evening	law		
everyone	Lord		
Exodus	manna		
follow	moaned		
full	morning		
given	Moses		
God	murmured		

Hidden Message:

_____

_____

_____

_____

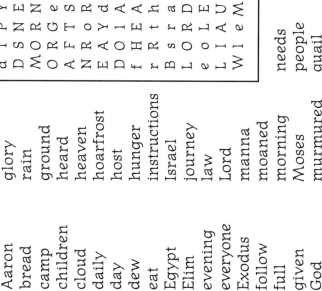

Then the Lord said to Moses, "I will rain down bread from heaven for you. The people are to go out each day and gather enough for that day. In this way I will test them and see whether they will follow my instructions."

Exodus 16:4

These are pictures of what manna may have looked like:

Children's Bulletin

This model may be similar to a section of a wall of the tabernacle. It will give you an idea of GOD'S GREAT DESIGN in every detail of the tabernacle.

Each board, made of strong shittim wood, had strong brass rings that round rods would slip through, thus holding it together with other boards.

The boards and rods could be taken apart and packed for transport.

The bars were staggered for strength. How is that for the first portable church!

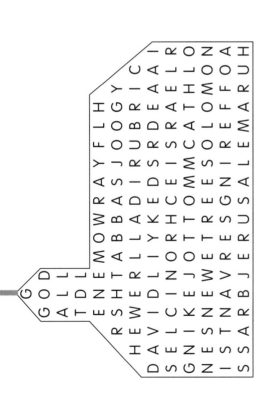

```
G
G O D
A L L
T D L
E N E M O W R A Y F L H
R S H T A B B A S J O O G Y
H E W E R L L A D I R U B R I C
D A V I D L I Y K E D S R D E A A I
S E L C I N O R H C E I S R A E L R
G N I K E J O T T O M M C A T H L O
N E S N E W E T R E E S O L O M O N
I S T N A V R E S G N I R E F F O A
S S A R B J E R U S A L E M A R U H
```

Words for Word Find:

all	gold	Judah	sings
brass	great	King	skill
cedar	hewer	linen	Solomon
Chronicles	house	Lord	trees
David	huram	men	women
fourscore	iron	oil	work
gates	Israel	sabbaths	
gems	Jerusalem	servants	
God	joy	silver	

Answers
to Tabernacle Terms:
(1) *Ropes*   (2) *Curtains*
(3) *Basin*   (4) *Pegs*
(5) *Acacia*   (6) *Clasps*

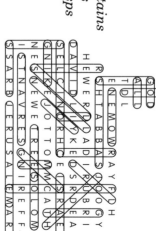

Exodus 35:4

Moses said to the whole Israelite community, "This is what the Lord has commanded."

Tabernacle Terms

By checking the verses from Exodus 35 you can find which part of the tabernacle is described. Write the words in the blanks.

Ropes   Pegs   Clasps   Curtains   Acacia   Basin

1. _____ were fastened to the pegs of the tabernacle. The strongest of these were made of strips of camel hide (v. 18).

2. _____ separated the rooms of the tabernacle, since there were no doors or walls. One curtain was 42 feet long and 6 feet wide (v. 17).

3. _____ was a special vessel used only by the priests (v. 16).

4. _____ were most often made of copper and driven into the ground to hold the ropes of the tabernacle (v. 18).

5. _____ was a very hard and durable wood. It was tough, with a close grain, and brown in color (v. 7).

6. _____ were fastenings made of gold and brass connecting the curtains or hangings of the tabernacle (v. 1).

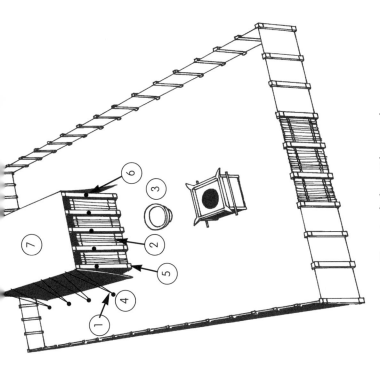

Portable Church

This is a sketch of the tabernacle. The numbers will identify some of the tabernacle parts mentioned Exodus 35:4–18.

1. **Ropes:** You can see why they had to be very strong and durable to hold up the tabernacle.
2. **Curtains:** beautiful, hand-woven linen, hand-embroidered in gold.
3. **Basin:** This was a very special basin used by priests for washing.
4. **Pegs:** stakes to hold the ropes.
5. **Acacia wood:** strong and durable.
6. **Clasps:** held back the curtains.
7. **Ram skins and hides of sea cows:** sewn together for the covering of the tabernacle.

Children's Bulletin

Thought:

Joshua made it plain and clear,
serving his God he loved so dear.
The choice is yours.

Find Joshua 24:15 and fill in the letters
as you follow each word in the verse.
This is an acrostic puzzle—THE CHOICE IS YOURS, but if
serving the Lord seems undesirable to you, ...

	then ☐ hoose for yourselves
	t ☐ is day
	wh ☐ m
	you w ☐ ll serve, whether
	☐ h your
	the gods whi ☐
	forefathers serv ☐ d beyond
	the R ☐ ver,
	or the god ☐ of the Amorites
	in whose land ☐ ou are living.
	But as f ☐ r me
	and my ho ☐ sehold,
	we will se ☐ ve the Lord.
	Based on Jo ☐ shua 24:15

God Closes and Opens Doors

Skeeter scoots under a lot of doors. Here are four doors. Can you find where they go in the mini story?

1

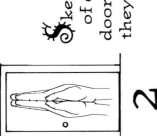

2

3

4

Home is a place where the great are small and the small are great.

Boys and girls, all houses have doors. We go in and come out of doors. Doors are important openings. There is a door for us to use each morning, or any time of the day. When we open this door we talk to Jesus. _____ As you learn about Jesus. Jesus, you will want him as your Savior and special friend. When that happens you'll open this special door. _____

Look at the doors in your home. Sometimes the outside doors look like like this one. Some churches have doors that look like this door. Its design will remind you of the cross where Jesus died._____

There is one door we sometimes shut because we hide secret things—like sin—there that we don't want anyone to know about. Sometimes the door seems to lock like a _____ door. Let Jesus use his special key of love and forgiveness to release you from behind that door.

God always gives his best to those who leave the CHOICE with him.

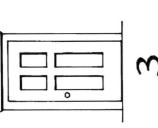

As for me and my house-hold, we will serve the Lord.

Prayer is the key of the morning and the bolt of night.

Matthew Henry

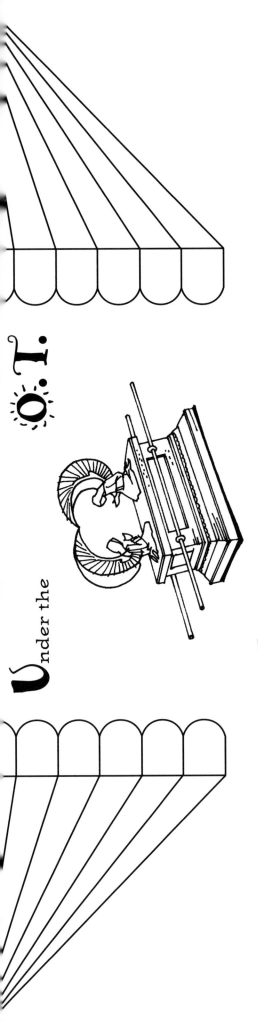

Under the O. T.

All about the ark: It was the first piece of furniture for the tabernacle. It was a box made of acacia wood, overlaid with gold. It was lined with gold. A ring was on each of its four upper corners. Each ring was covered with gold. The rods that fit through the rings were also covered with gold. There are two golden cherubims mounted on the top, facing each other.

The ark was a very special chest. Who do you think designed it?

In 2 Samuel 6:1–11, doing right the wrong way was David's decision. In today's message can you tell what David did wrong? Fill in blanks with   Yes or No

Did 30,000 chosen men make a grand parade of praise? _____

Did the music with all those instruments please God? _____

Was God pleased with David for moving the ark? _____

More about the ark: Who designed it? God. What was kept in the ark? The ark may have had the tablets of the law (Ten Commandments), the rod of Aaron, and perhaps the likeness of a pot of manna in it. It was a sacred chest, which is what ark means. It was kept in the Holy of Holies in the tabernacle.

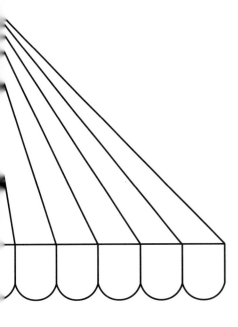

From the Greatest

No reserved seats

A ringside seat for everyone

Skeeter's grammar is poor, but he wanted to try to disguise the names of some Old Testament books of the Bible. Can you find them hidden in the sentences he wrote? Underline the names when you find them.

Example: *David, the king, sings when he plays his harp.*

1. Formica has a hard surface.
2. That old nag, "Hag," gaits so slow.
3. I'm ala chicken eater myself.
4. He's the right man to do the job.
5. Blue genes is OK to wear.
6. Can, I eliminate the onions first.
7. Na—hum any time you please.
8. O bad! I ah, "oh" my, I'm frustrated.
9. A hose: a long thing to sprinkle lawns with.
10. This is a most exciting book—read it.
11. I can prove R. B. said that!
12. He can solo; money is no object.
13. Juru, the man from India, stopped by.
14. Lez rather read than play games

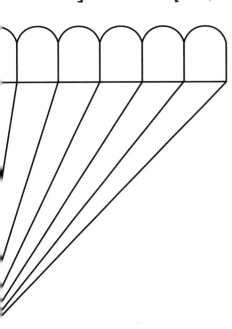

Book on Earth!

All ages

1 1/2 hours

Children's Bulletin

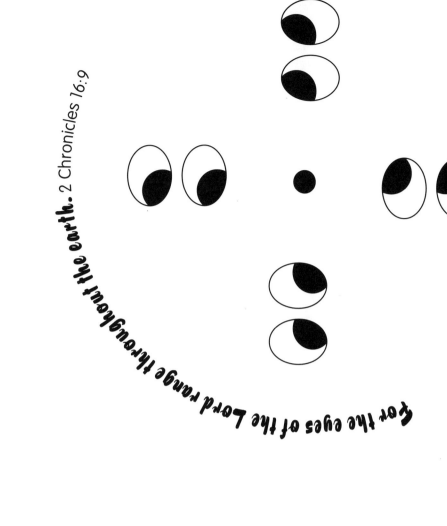

For the eyes of the Lord range throughout the earth. 2 Chronicles 16:9

Eyes

Without our vision we could not read in the Bible how the Lord watches over the earth. We need our eyes.

This may be a good time to introduce you to the **concordance** of your Bible. The **concordance** is a special part of your Bible where you can look up words such as eyes. It will tell you where you can find verses in the Bible with the word eyes in them. Ask Mom and Dad to teach you how to use a **concordance**.

Just for fun (and for learning, too) look up the word eyes. See how many verses there are? To learn more about what your Bible says about eyes, take some time and look up some or all of the verses. Write them in a notebook. Try to memorize a few, especially 2 Chronicles 16:9.

For the eyes of the Lord range throughout the earth to strengthen those who are fully committed to him. 2 Chronicles 16:9a

Answers:
(A) Paul   (B) Joshua   (C) Isaiah   (D) John the Baptist
(E) Jesus   (F) Moses   (G) Samuel   (H) Jesus

"I" service . . .

Here are some I's from some special people. Look up these verses. Match them and find the names to fill in the blanks. **Who said:**

Exodus 4:10—Moses

Revelation 3:20—Jesus

1 Samuel 3:10—Samuel

Isaiah 6:8—Isaiah

John 14:6—Jesus

Joshua 24:15—Joshua

John 3:30—John the Baptist

Romans 1:16—Paul

A. I am not ashamed of the gospel.

B. As for me and my household, we will serve the Lord.

C. I heard the voice of the Lord saying, "Whom shall I send? And who will go for us?" Then I said, "Here am I. Send me."

D. He must become greater; I must become less.

E. Here I am! I stand at the door and knock.

F. O Lord, I have never been eloquent, neither in the past nor since you have spoken to your servant. I am slow of speech and tongue.

G. Speak, for your servant is listening.

H. I am the way, the truth, and the life. No one comes to the Father except through me.

Walk in wisdom toward them that are without.

Redeeming the time • Colossians 4:5

11 12 1 2 3 4 5 6 7 8 9 10

Fill in the blanks with vowels that match the symbols in the code.

___t__ll y___ th__ r__s r__j__c__ng __n th__
pr__s__nc__ __f th__ __ng__ls __f G__d __v__r __n__
s__nn__r wh__ r__p__nts. Luke 15:10.

How many times can you find the word Joy in this bulletin? _____

Did you see and sing the word Joy in the hymns you sang today? How many times? _____

Listen to your pastor and count the times he uses the word Joy in the scripture and in his sermon message. _____

Th__ t__j__y __s m__n__. John 3:29

___nd h__ w__ll br__ng j__y t__ __ll n__t__ __ns. Isaiah 42:1

Joy is multiplied as it is divided with others.

J__y __nd gl__dn__ss. Joel 1:16

J—Jesus first
O—Others second
Y—Yourself last

Th__ L__rd __s kn__wn by h__s j__y Psalm 9:16

Is there enough joy in this bulletin for you today?

Joy: the mark of Christianity.

A E I O U

I BRING YOU good

Joy Word Find

Find the words from all the joy verses, including the books the verses are from. One very special word not listed is rejoicing, but you can find joy four times!

```
Y O J L L E T
Y H O U L N H
Y U H K I I E
O N E W M
Y J A L L
A M A F O
S S N Y R
P S G O D
R E E J N
E N L H A
S D S A T
E A B I I
N L R A O
B E C G I S N
H A T R E N N I S
T K N O W N G H
```

	his	mine	tell
	in	nations	that
	is	of	the
all	Isaiah	one	there
and	John	over	to
angels	known	presence	who
bring	Lord	Psalm	will
by	Luke	sinner	you
gladness			
God			
he			

NEWS OF GREAT

BIBLE CLOSET

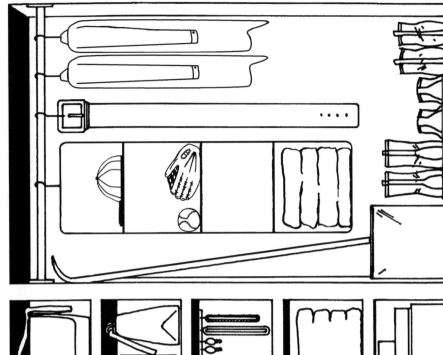

Rearrange the scrambled words.

1. RIDEGL
2. LIPWEMS
3. FFATS
4. BETLAST
5. PRANO
6. SULAC
7. SNIP SPINGRIC
8. NEATLM
9. KOLAC
10. SHINAC
11. HODO
12. ANDLASS
13. LUMFFRE
14. SIRET

Fuller's Trade
Malachi 3:2

Stone Washed

The Bible closet may have clothes similar to what we wear today . . .

See how many items you can match

MIX AND MATCH

Today's Clothes

1. underwear
2. coat
3. scarf
4. shoes
5. belts
6. cane
7. jewelry
8. headdress
9. turban
10. shawls
11. bonnet
12. bracelets
13. robe
14. mourning robe
15. purse (fanny pack)

Bible Apparel

A. sandals—Mark 6:9
B. chains—Isaiah 3:19
C. staff—Mark 6:8
D. crisping pins—Isaiah 3:22
E. sackcloth—2 Samuel 3:31
F. wimples—Isaiah 3:22
G. apron—Genesis 3:7
H. tablets—Isaiah 3:20
I. muffler—Isaiah 3:19
J. hood—Isaiah 3:23
K. cloak—Luke 6:29
L. mantle—Isaiah 3:22
M. girdle—1 Kings 2:13
N. tires—Isaiah 3:18
O. cauls—Isaiah 3:18

Holy Bible
Weavers of Wool
Fullers' Handbook
Ornamental clothiers
Spinners and Tanners
Embroidery Vol. 1
Embroidery Vol. 2
Bible Occupations
Needle Work of Women
The Tailor's Thread
Early Garments

Stone washed clothes are not a new idea! Malachi 3:2 and Mark 9:3 speak of the "fuller" and of "fuller's soap." A fuller prepared skins by washing them with soap, pounding, and shrinking them.

Crisping pins may well be the forerunner of what are now called "fanny packs." Women wore them as purses in concealed places or as an ornamental part of their outfit.

Tires (Ezekiel 24:17 KJV) and mufflers were not automobile parts. They were bonnets and scarves.

Be sure to read Isaiah 3:18–23, which uses these three terms. It's an interesting passage. Compare these verses in both the King James Version and the New International Version. Notice the change in words.

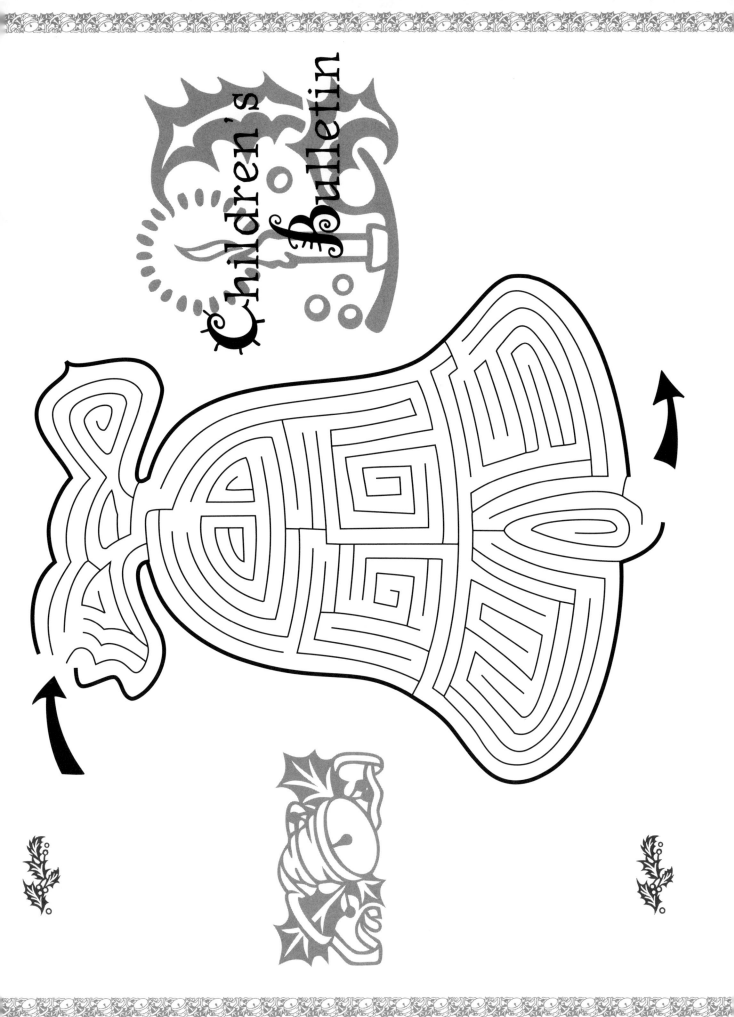

Children's Bulletin

Put the letters in the matching blanks

Gospel Bells[△]

Gospel Bells,
Gospel Bells,
Ring them all the day.
Ring them while you're
at your work,
And while you're at
your play.
Oh . . .
Gospel Bells,
Gospel Bells,
Ring them all the day.
Ring out the news that
Jesus came
To take our sins
away!

[△]Sing to the tune of *Jingle Bells*.

1. $\frac{8}{A}$ $\frac{1}{C}$ $\frac{2}{H}$ $\frac{6}{T}$ $\frac{4}{T}$ $\frac{3}{S}$

   ___ ___ ___ ___ ___ ___ ___ ___
   1 2 3 4 5 6 7 8 5

2. $\frac{3}{N}$ $\frac{2}{A}$ $\frac{5}{E}$ $\frac{6}{R}$ $\frac{7}{M}$ $\frac{5}{S}$ $\frac{4}{G}$ $\frac{1}{W}$

   ___ ___ ___ ___ ___ ___
   1 2 3 4 5 6

3. ___ ___ ___ ___ ___
   1 2 3 4 5

4. ___ ___ ___ ___ ___ ___ ___ ___ ___
   6 7 4 8 7 4 9 10 6

5. ___ ___ ___ ___ ___ ___ ___ ___
   3 11 11 10   2 4 12 6

$\frac{4}{E}$ $\frac{1}{A}$ $\frac{2}{N}$ $\frac{5}{L}$ $\frac{9}{R}$ $\frac{8}{P}$

$\frac{3}{G}$ $\frac{10}{D}$ $\frac{11}{O}$ $\frac{12}{W}$ $\frac{7}{H}$ $\frac{6}{S}$

300 CUBITS LONG

LOWER FLOOR

SECOND FLOOR

FIRST FLOOR

30 CUBITS HIGH

Noah's Ark

CHILDREN'S BULLETIN

If you can find ten, you are a very good word-maker!

How many two-, three-, and four-letter words can you make from the letters in THE FLOOD?

he, food, hood, dot, hot, lot, foot, to, too, tool, do, led, fed, fled, loft, oft, lode, ode, deft, heft, left

Answers:
(1) Noah
(2) Noah, Ham, Shem, Japeth
(3) cypress wood
(4) pitch
(5) 40
(6) 150
(7) 450, 75, 45 (or 300 cubits long, 50 cubits wide, 30 cubits high).
(8) to destroy all the wicked people

Find all the answers in the first book of the Bible—Genesis. Read chapters 6 and 7.

1. GOD SPOKE TO _____

2. _____ had three sons whose names were, (6:10) _____ _____ and _____

3. Build an _____ (6:14)

Build the ark with _____ (6:14)

4. Put it together with _____ (6:14)

5. It rained how many _____ days? (7:12)

6. But the flood lasted _____ days (7:24)

7. How long was the ark? _____ cubits or _____ feet.

How wide was the ark? _____ cubits or _____ feet.

How high was the ark? _____ cubits or _____ feet (6:15) (KJV) (NIV)

8. Why did God send a flood to destroy the whole earth? (6:5–7)

CHILDREN'S BULLETIN

JERICHO WALL
Joshua 6:1-20

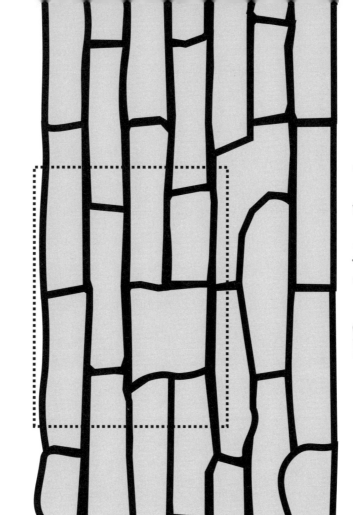

Come, little children, and listen today.
Hear Joshua's story and how he obeyed.

Joshua was reassured by the commander of the Lord's army. These fun letters form special words from this passage.

1. _ _ _ _ _ _

2. _ _ _ _

3. _ _ _ _

4. _ _ _ _ _

5. _ _ _ _ _ _ _

6. _ _ _ _

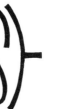     

7. _ _ _ _ _ _ _ _ _

Joshua commanded all the [people] not 2 shout

nor make any sound, nor words 2 come from

your [mouth] until the day [eye] bid U shout, then

you shall **SHOUT.**

Joshua marched quietly [around the city] in the morning and with

7 priests. This was on day 1 . . . again on day 2 . . .

again on day 3 . . . again on day 4, so quietly as com-

manded . . . again on day 5 . . . again on day 6.

But on day 7 the 7 priests with 7 [trumpet]s and

armed men and all the [people] marched [around the city] 7

[horn]'s and on the 7th X the priests blew a

LONG blast on the 7 [horn]'s and all

the [people] **SHOUTED,**

"4 the Lord has given U the city!"

Now reach up and pull the wall down flat.

JERICHO was shut [up] [arrow]-cause no 1 came

[in] and no 1 went [out]. The **LORD** spoke

to Joshua, "Go [around the city] once 4 six days with 7 priests

[bee] 4 the ark of the covenant and [bear]ing a [horn].

But on the 7th day, march [around the city] 7 X's [blowing] the

[horn] 7th X. And when U H+[ear] the **LONG**

blast with the [horn], the [people] will shout and the

walls of the city shall fall **FLAT!**

Proverbs can be called the book of wisdom. A proverb is a wise saying that can help us decide what is the best thing to do.

Some short proverbs are hidden in these word patterns. Can you unscramble them?

Here's one clue:　**K** —speak up
　　　　　　　　　A
　　　　　　　　　E
　　　　　　　　　P
　　　　　　　　　S

1. E
　　R
　　O my commands
　　T within you
　　S

2. Y
　　L
　　T
　　G
　　I
　　R
　　P
　　U

　　K
　　L
　　A
　　W

3.　　STAND
　　　RIGHTEOUSNESS

4.　　　O V
　　　Lall wrongs **E**

5. Knowledge
　　Wise Men

PROVERBS Rx
PHARMACY

"For wisdom will enter your heart, and knowledge will be pleasant to your soul. Discretion will protect you, and understanding will guard you."
Proverbs 2:10–11

Rx: 2x a day (Rx means take thou, and is used before a medical pre-scription.)

#2 Proverbial Pill
100 mg. 4 U (full strength)
Refill often

Warning: Use with care; this Scripture is not to be taken lightly.

Answers:

(1) G　1. *Store up my com-*
(2) D　　*mands within you.*
(3) C　2. *Walk uprightly.*
(4) E　3. *Understand*
(5) H　　*righteousness.*
(6) F　4. *Love covers all wrongs.*
(7) B　5. *Wise men lay up*
(8) A　　*knowledge.*

What things are listed in our Bible that we would find in today's pharmacy, or drug store? Read over the list and try to match the Bible items with today's products.

Bible—Apothecary

1. cleansing mineral (Ezekiel 16:4)
2. alabaster (Matthew 26:7)
3. balm of Gilead (Jeremiah 8:22)
4. molten-looking glass (Job 37:18)
5. soda(nitre) (Jeremiah 2:22)
6. scented oils (Psalm 45:8)
7. cleansing qualities (Malachi 3:2)
8. camphire (Song of Solomon 4:13)

Today—Pharmacy

A. henna (dye)
B. soap
C. eye salve
D. vases and jars (marble and onyx)
E. mirror
F. perfume
G. salt
H. lye

Children's Bulletin

H ere are the names of 13(?) disciples.
They are all scrambled up.
Unscramble them.

1. SHOMAT
2. SINMO HET AZELOT
3. WAREND
4. HOJN
5. MEAJS (brother of Jesus)
6. DUSAJ ROICASIT _____
7. PIPHIL
8. SADUJ
9. WHATTME
10. NISMO TREEP
11. SEAMJ (of Alphaeus)
12. LANANATHE
13. UYRO ENMA *

Fishers of Men

Jesus had twelve disciples, and three of them were fishermen. Look up Mark 1:19 and find the other two. 1. Andrew 2._____ 3._____. Jesus took these three men and taught them all the ways about God, and they became fishers of men!

Matthew 17:27 has an interesting story about a special fish with a special _____. *Well, you read it and find out for yourself.* Jesus said to Simon, "go to the lake and throw out your line. Take the first fish you catch _____; open_____. _____Did that surprise you to find out what was in the fish's mouth?

Another fish story is found in John 21:4–6. That was some catch! Jesus spoke and it was so. How many fish this time, boys and girls? a _____ number.

Hidden letters in this fish will spell the name of a special fisherman.

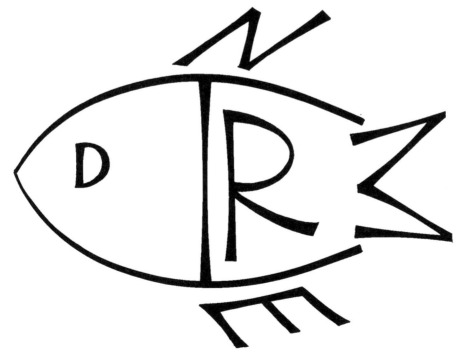

Children's Bulletin

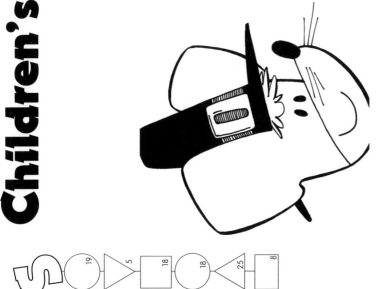

Skeeter says

"Thank you for coming" to all the boys and girls. It just tickles him all over to see those smiling faces each week.

Column 1

What are you thankful for?

Code for Thanks

1. A	14. N
2. B	15. O
3. C	16. P
4. D	17. Q
5. E	18. R
6. F	19. S
7. G	20. T
8. H	21. U
9. I	22. V
10. J	23. W
11. K	24. X
12. L	25. Y
13. M	26. Z

THANKS

1- 10 19 5 19 21 5
2- 2 2 9 20 12 5 18
3- 6 20 1 15 8 5 18
4- 13 13 1 20 9 8 18
5- 6 6 1 5 12 25 3
6- 3 8 18 18 3 8 18

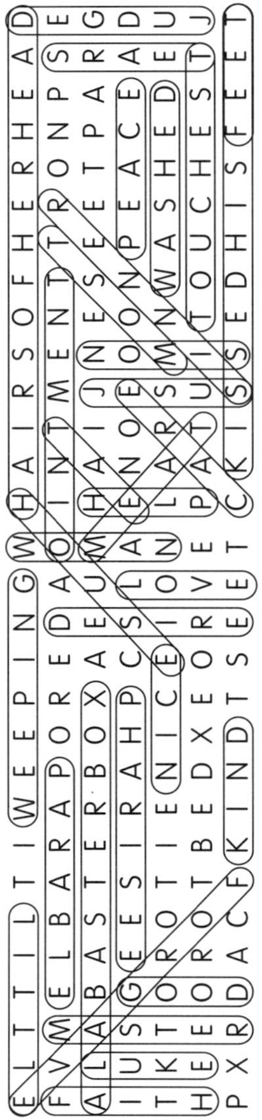

Answers:

To Thanks puzzle
1. Jesus
2. Bible
3. Father
4. Mother
5. Family
6. Church

Column 1

Can you think of more things to be thankful for?

1. _____
2. _____
3. _____
4. _____
5. _____
6. _____

Demonstrating

```
E L T L T I W E E P I N G W H A I R S O F H E R H E A D
F V M E L B A R A P O R E D A O I N T M E N T T R O N P S E
A L A B A S T E R B O X A E U M H A I J N E S E E T P A R G
I U S G E E S I R A H P C S L A E N O E O O N P E A C E A D
T K T O R O T I E N I C E I O N L A R S M N W A S H E D E U
H E E O R O T B E D X E O R V E P A T U I T O U C H E S T J
P X R D A C E F I N D T S E E T C K I S S E D H I S F E E T
```

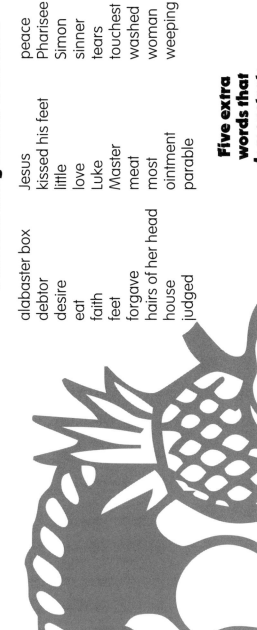

Demonstrating thanks word find:

alabaster box	Jesus	peace
debtor	kissed his feet	Pharisee
desire	little	Simon
eat	love	sinner
faith	Luke	tears
feet	Master	touchest
forgave	meat	washed
hairs of her head	most	woman
house	ointment	weeping
judged	parable	

Five extra words that demonstrate thanks:

care
good
help
kind
nice

Cut this dark section away

Cut line

The caterpillar is mentioned in the Bible. As a reminder of the plagues, Psalm 78:46 says, "He gave also their increase unto the caterpillar." (Also check out Isaiah 33:4; 1 Kings 8:37; Jeremiah 51:27.) All verses are from the King James Version. If you want this caterpillar to grow up and be a . . .

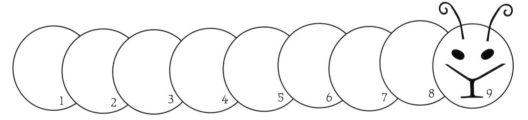

. . . answer these questions below.

1. If you ask a lot of questions, put <u>Y</u> in circle #9.
2. If you tease little kids (shame on you), put <u>T</u> in circle #4.
3. Put <u>U</u> in circle #2 if you went to bed on time last night.
4. Are you listening to the sermon? If yes, put <u>L</u> in circle #8.
5. If you learned a memory verse this week, put <u>E</u> in circle #5.
6. If you have good Sunday School attendance, put <u>R</u> in circle #6.
7. If you put your toys away without being told, put <u>T</u> in circle #3.
8. Put <u>F</u> in circle #7 if you sing all the hymns today.
9. Did you eat a good breakfast this morning? Put <u>B</u> in circle #1 if you did.

Acrostic
answers:
1. those
2. who
3. believe
4. blessed
5. are

esus told him, "Because you have seen me, you have believed; blessed are those who have not seen and yet have believed.

John 20:29

Here are words Jesus said, but jumbled:

Fit these words into the acrostic. Start with #1.

Now can you put the words in the correct order?

__ __ E __ __ E __ __ __ E

__ __ __ __ __ E __ __ __ __ __ E __ __ E __ E.

are   who

blessed believed

those

have

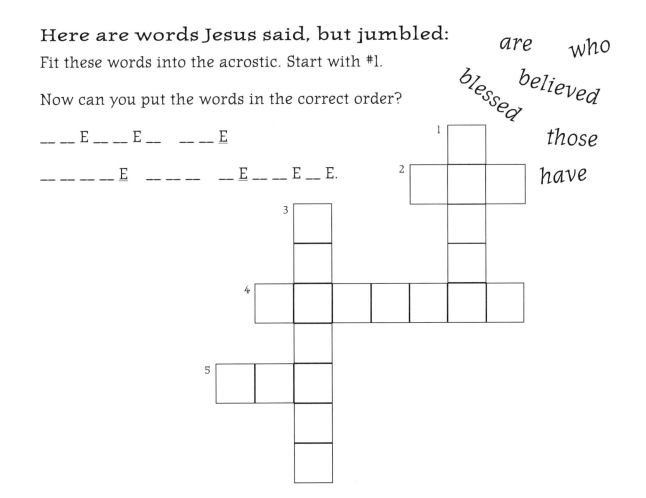

APOKALUPSIS*

*Greek word for REVELATION—to uncover, lift up a curtain for all to see

ALPHA

OMEGA

Find some vital words from Revelation 1:1–18 (KJV)

angels
Asia
candlesticks
churches
Ephesus
evil
first
four
God
hear
John
Laodicia
write

love
Lord
Patmos
Pergamos
Philadelphia
revelation
Sardis
seven
Smyrna
Spirit
stars
Thyatira

```
S U S E H P E T
P E R G A M O S
H A W R I T E M
I S T O A V T Y
L R E M E L S R
A A R N O A R N
D T E R A S I A
E S D S H U F S
L K J E F O U R
P C O H R S A N
H I H C E E R O
I T N R H V I I
A S P U S I T T
N E A H S L A A
G L E C P O Y L
E D O G I V H E
L N W S R E T V
S A R D I S O E
M C O N T E N R
L A O D I C I A
```

Answers:
Missing letter—U, to form the word 'churches'.

And the seven candlesticks which thou sawest are the seven churches.

Revelation 1:20, KJV

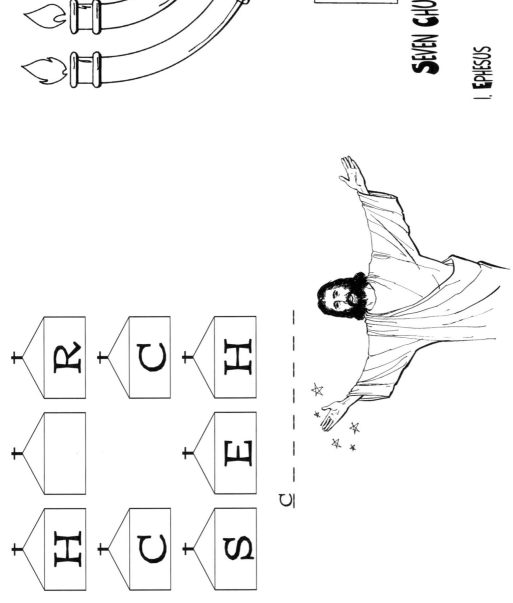

Verse 11 lists the seven churches. Put the name of one in each candlestick.

SEVEN CHURCHES

1. EPHESUS
2. SMYRNA
3. PERGAMOS
4. THYATIRA
5. SARDIS
6. PHILADELPHIA
7. LAODICEA

The churches below want to spell something. What letter is missing?

H   R

C   C   C

S   E   H

C _ _ _ _ _

I AM LORD!

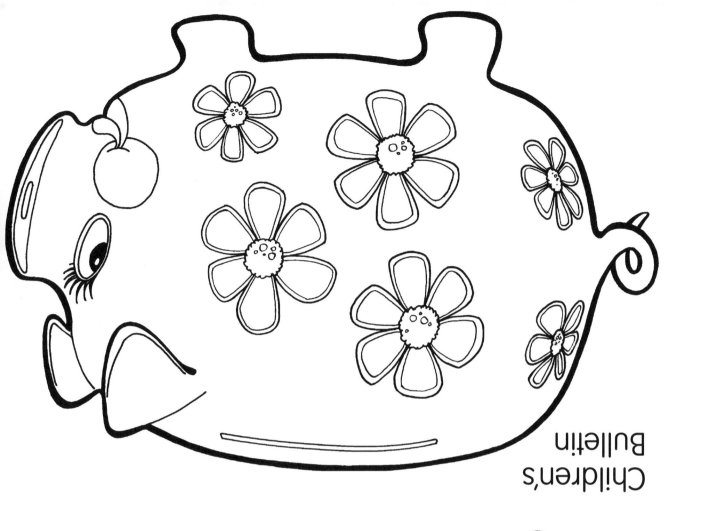

Children's Bulletin

IS THE RIVER ALWAYS RICH?

each week! Thank$ kid$!

WHAT DID ONE PENNY $AY TO THE OTHER PENNY?

Dollar$ go much farther when accompanied by ene.

Dear $keeter,

I think I am old enough to have an allowance. Mom and Dad $ay no. They want me to work around the hou$e for nothing.

Earn E.

Dear Earn E.,

Money i$n't everything. You are learning a valuable le$$on when you help around the hou$e. $keeter

BANK TONGUE TWI$TER $AY FA$T $EVERAL TIME$: "**B**ABYLON BANK$ BARGAIN BASKET$ OF BLUE BILL$."

FROM OUR BIRTHDAY BANK VAULT OF GOOD WIHE:

Answers
to riddles:
(1) It has a river bank on each side.
(2) Lets get together and make cents.

ALL ABOUT BANKS...

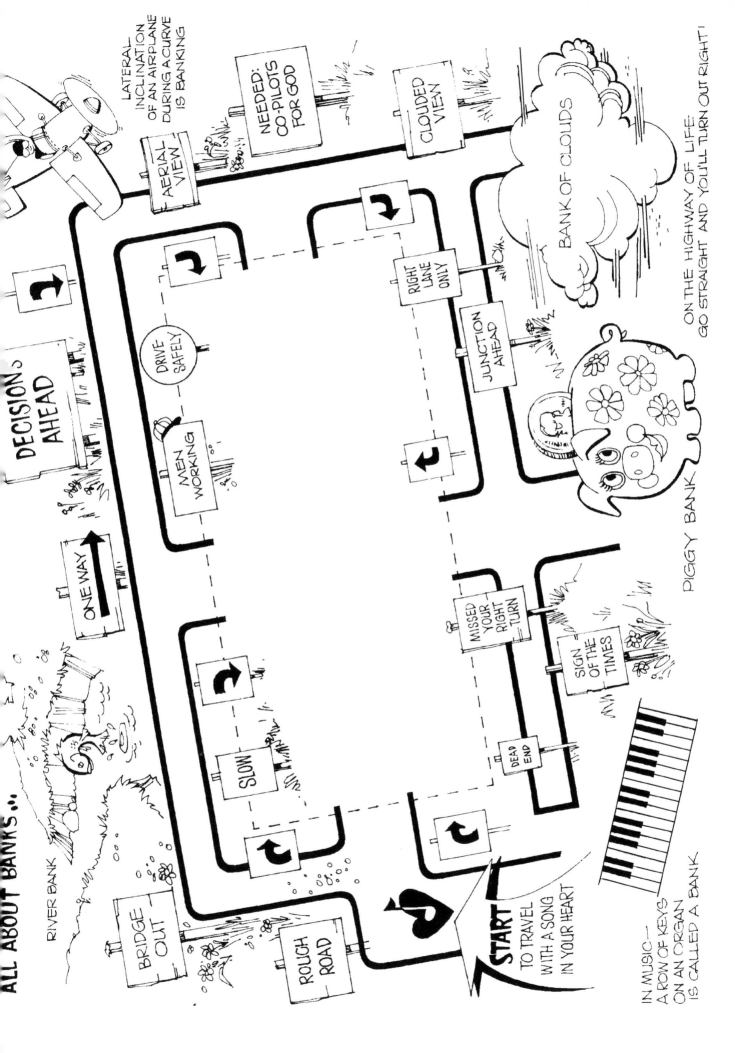

LATERAL INCLINATION OF AN AIRPLANE DURING A CURVE IS BANKING

NEEDED: CO-PILOTS FOR GOD

AERIAL VIEW

CLOUDED VIEW

BANK OF CLOUDS

ON THE HIGHWAY OF LIFE, GO STRAIGHT AND YOU'LL TURN OUT RIGHT!

DECISIONS AHEAD

RIVER BANK

DRIVE SAFELY

ONE WAY

MEN WORKING

RIGHT LANE ONLY

JUNCTION AHEAD

PIGGY BANK

SLOW

MISSED YOUR RIGHT TURN

DEAD END

SIGN OF THE TIMES

BRIDGE OUT

ROUGH ROAD

START
TO TRAVEL WITH A SONG IN YOUR HEART

IN MUSIC—
A ROW OF KEYS ON AN ORGAN IS CALLED A BANK

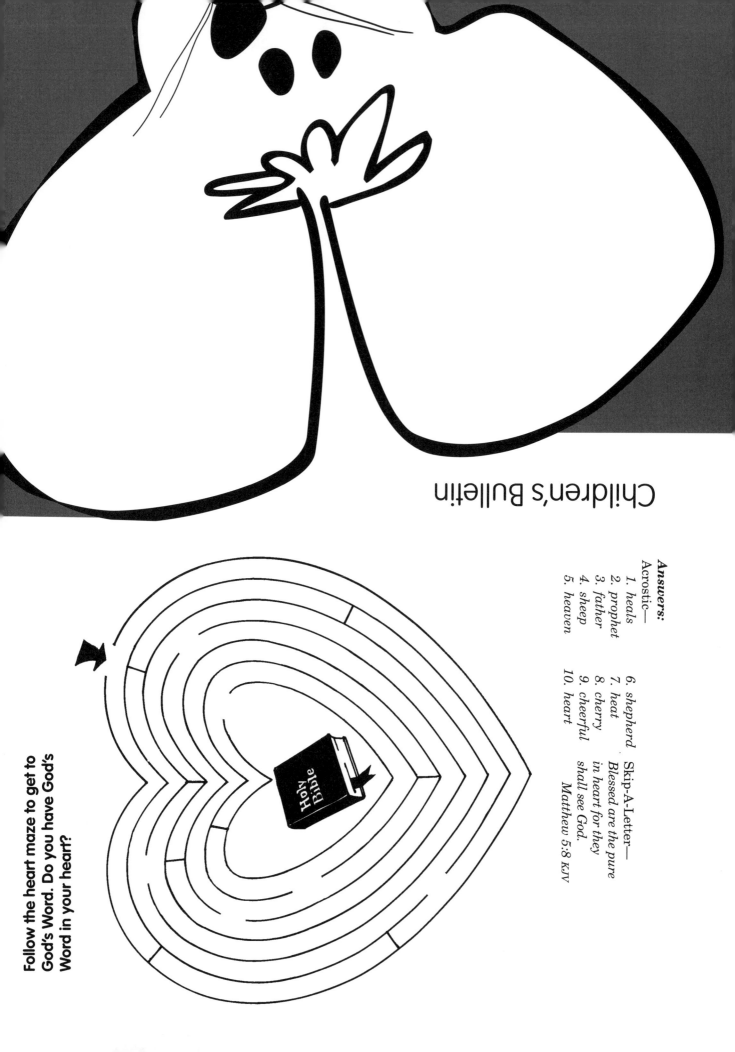

Children's Bulletin

Follow the heart maze to get to God's Word. Do you have God's Word in your heart?

Answers:
Acrostic—
1. heals
2. prophet
3. father
4. sheep
5. heaven
6. shepherd
7. heat
8. cherry
9. cheerful
10. heart

Skip-A-Letter—
Blessed are the pure
in heart for they
shall see God.
Matthew 5:8 KJV

Matthew 5:8 (KJV)

Skip-a-Letter Heart

Start with B at the arrow and go around to every other letter. Put those letters in the blanks within the heart. Go around twice without starting over.

Acrostic Heart

1. Something the Lord does for us (Exodus 15:26)
2. Special men of God (Luke 24:19)
3. Another name for Dad
4. An animal (Psalm 100:3)
5. A special place (2 Chronicles 2:6)
6. Found in Psalm 23:1
7. Cold and ___ (Genesis 8:22)
8. A little red fruit
9. A word in Proverbs 15:13
10. Hide God's Word here (Psalm 119:11)

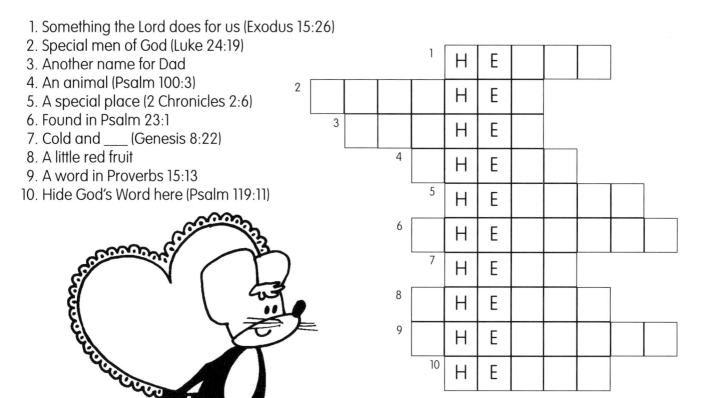

God created everything. God created the cold, hail, frost, ice, snow, and winter. Well, boys and girls, let's pretend to put on our boots, warm jacket, hat, and scarf and search for these chilly words in the Bible!

a. cold   b. hail   c. frost   d. ice   e. snow   f. winter

Write one of the words in each blank to complete the verses below.

1. Exodus 16:14: . . . thin flakes like _____ on the ground appeared.

2. Exodus 9:18: I will send the worst _____ storm that has ever fallen on Egypt.

3. 2 Samuel 23:20: He also went down into a pit on a _____y day.

4. Job 6:16: When darkened by thawing _____ and swollen with melting _____.

5. Psalm 147:16: He spreads the _____ like wool and scatters the _____ like ashes.

6. Jeremiah 36:22: The king was sitting in the _____ apartment.

7. Psalm 147:17: He hurls down his _____ like pebbles. Who can stand his icy blast?

Where do snowmen keep their money?

Glue

Glue Here

Glue

Use the code below to fill in the spaces in the snow fort and find a special verse.

Code:

1-B	2-A	3-E	4-H	5-D	6-L	7-I
8-S	9-N	10-O	11-R	12-M	13-T	14-W

Unscramble the names below to find key people in Christ's birth.

1. Ryam _____   5. Nojh _____

2. Sujes _____   6. Peohjs _____

3. Baliteezh _____   7. Rehdshsep _____

4. Hichazare _____

Fill in the blanks with the words hidden in these fun-letter pictures.

1. _ _ _ _ _ _

2. _ _ _ _ _

3. _ _ _ _ _ _

4. _ _ _ _

J
A E C
G E S D F
B U H
E A S T C
E I B D J G K
L N E M E S I W M
M N C H F
K E S R E T Y
I O H A E P S P R
N Q T E V E H S U R A
G Y V Z L I H E R O D W M
H H O X R B A
P C T R E D D F N
E G H E A S S H J L G
S M G K B S T A X E D L E
O O I S P T M A N G E R Q U L
J R N F L O C K R P I H S R O W V
J O Y
I N N

ANGEL	GIFTS	KING	SON
BABE	HEROD	MANGER	STAR
BETHLEHEM	INN	MARY	TAXED
DECREE	JESUS	NIGHT	WISEMEN
EAST	JOSEPH	SAVIOR	WORSHIP
FLOCK	JOY	SHEPHERDS	

Here are words that can be found in Luke 2:1–7. Draw a line to the correct answer.

1. decree   a. promised to marry

2. lineage   b. a place to stay

3. swaddling   c. an order or law

4. taxed   d. strips of long cloth

5. espoused   e. family

6. inn   f. have to pay money

Color the squares that are blank and find a special name. (Hint: we're celebrating his birthday TODAY!)

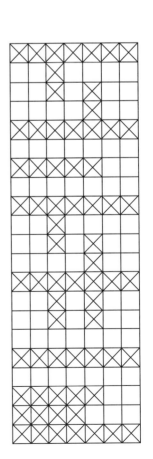

Fun Facts

Buttons were worn by Egyptians thousands of years ago. The Egyptians used buttons as ornaments, not to hold parts of clothing together.

Hook and eyes were invented by Whitcomb Judson in 1893 to fasten pieces of clothing together.

Zippers were invented in 1913 by Gideon Sunback. The G. F. Goodrich Company designed rubber boots to put zippers in.

Velcro was designed in 1948 by a Swiss inventor who got the idea from looking at thistle seeds under a microscope. He saw that each seed had tiny hooklike pieces that made the seeds cling to clothing.

What other things do we use in our clothing? Snaps, shoe laces, belts, and buckles are a few.

In Bible times people wore **mantles**, a square piece of cloth with a hole cut in the center and a slit down the middle to provide the front opening. The sides were sewn part way up to form armholes. Often mantles were used as blankets at night.

Girdles were wide and long pieces of fabric that were carefully folded before being tied around the waist. People could carry things such as knives, food, coins, or even a small sword in the folds of the girdle.

A **tunic** was made almost like a mantle but without the slit down the middle. It was worn under the mantle.

Sandals were almost like the flip-flops we wear at the beach today, but they were made of leather. People removed them as a sign of reverence when an important person was speaking. When God spoke to Moses at the burning bush, the first thing God said to him was "Take off your shoes."

Draw a picture of a mantle, a tunic, and sandals.

Answers:
1—robe;
2—sandals;
3—robe;
4—robe;
5—undergarment;
6—clothes;

7—cloths;
8—ring, sandals;
9—purse, bag, sandals;
10—breastpiece, ephod, robe, tunic, turban, sash.

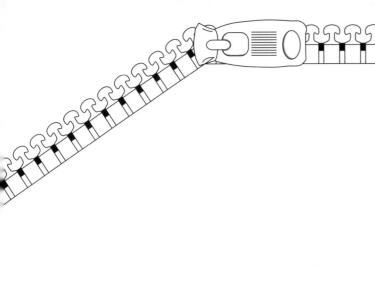

Fill in the blanks below with the name of an article of clothing. How many blanks could you fill in without looking up the answer in the Bible?

1. David cut off a piece of Saul's _____ (1 Samuel 24:4).

2. God told Isaiah to take the _____ off his feet (Isaiah 20:2).

3. Hannah made Samuel a little _____ (1 Samuel 2:19).

4. Jacob gave Joseph a beautiful _____ (Genesis 37:3).

5. Jesus had an _____ without a seam (John 19:23).

6. King Ahab tore his _____ (1 Kings 21:27).

7. Mary wrapped the baby Jesus in _____ (Luke 2:7).

8. The father put a _____ on the prodigal son's finger and _____ on his feet (Luke 15:22).

9. The disciples were sent out without _____ or _____ (Luke 22:35).

10. The high priest wore a _____ an _____ (apron), a _____ a woven _____ a _____ and a _____ (Exodus 28:4).

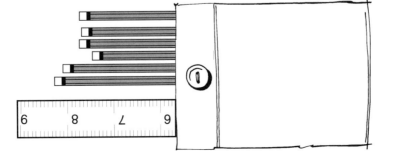

Children's Bulletin

The biggest trouble with sin is the "I" in the middle of it.

It is our intent to wish Happy Birthday to:

Attention: Today's helpers are:

Please pay attention to our prayer requests:

Something to think about:
Achan turned his content into a "con" -tent.

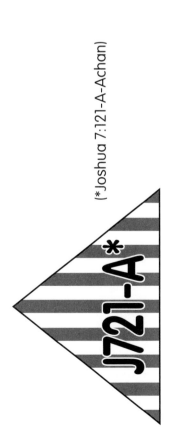

(*Joshua 7:121-A-Achan)

Something more to think about:

The trouble with a LITTLE SIN IS THAT IT WON'T STAY THAT WAY!

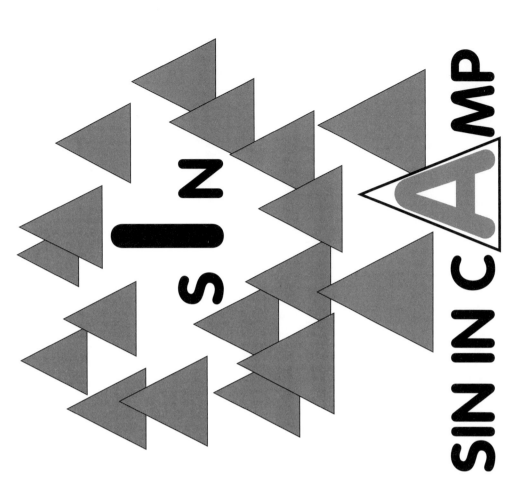

Answers
to Tents in Achan's Life:
(1) tents   (2) content   (3) intent
(4) tentatively (5) attention   (6) contention
(7) detention

Some Tents in Achan's Life*

Joshua sent his men to find Achan's tent. Can you find it through the maze?

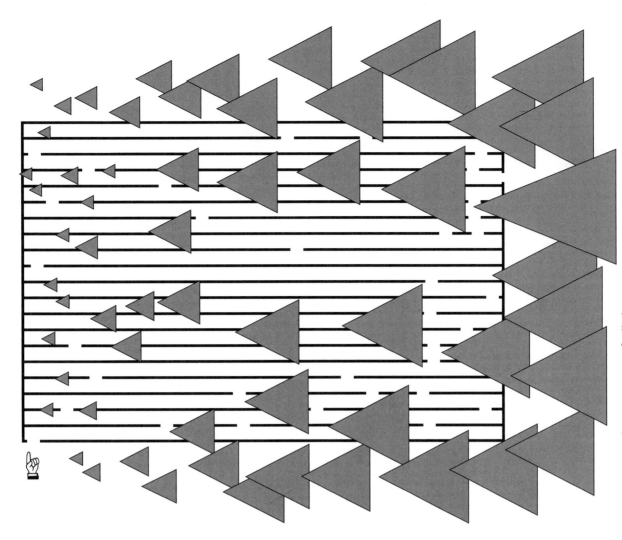

Sin is the greatest of all detectives.
Be sure it will **find you out.**

In these sentences you may find some words that are new to you. Each of these words has tent in it. Read each sentence carefully and look in the list and definitions below for which "tent" word belongs in that sentence.

1. The army of Joshua was encamped and living in <u>tent</u> _____.

2. Achan was not _____ <u>tent</u> _____ after attacking the enemies of Israel. __4__

3. Achan saw gold and silver, and it was his _____ <u>tent</u> to
   steal and hide it. __3__

4. Achan was not <u>tent</u> _____ _____ _____ dis-
   __1__ __3__ __2__
   obeying.

5. The Lord spoke to Joshua and brought it to his
   _____ <u>tent</u> _____ _____ that someone in the camp had
   __1__ __3__ __4__
   caused their defeat.

6. There was conflict in the army of Joshua, which caused
   _____ <u>tent</u> _____ _____ .
   __4__ __3__ __4__

7. Many good men were taken aside and questioned.
   Achan finally was questioned and held in
   _____ <u>tent</u> _____ _____ . He was punished by death.
   __2__ __3__ __4__

attention—thoughts   detention—being kept by yourself
content—happy or satisfied   intent—aim, plan
contention—struggling together   <u>tent</u>s—shelters made of fabric
and arguing   <u>tent</u>atively—unsure or hesitant

For a little extra help use this   <u>A E I O U</u>
vowel code. . . .   1 2 3 4 5

Children's Bulletin

What did a shepherd do? Find out by matching the words on the right to the left words on the left that finish the sentence.

1. In the morning he led

2. He was assisted

3. The sheep drink

4. If sheep strayed he

5. Arriving in the pasture he

6. In the evening he

a. from a running stream.

b. watched his flock.

c. would bring them back to the fold.

d. by dogs.

e. the flock from the fold.

f. would search for them.

Sheep and lambs have been mentioned many times in this bulletin. See how many times you can count the words <u>sheep</u> and <u>lamb</u>. _____ sheep _____ lamb

All about Shepherds

Young sheep are called lambs (Genesis 22:8). And when a male lamb learns to butt, he is called a ram (Genesis 22:13). A flock of sheep is first mentioned in Genesis 30:32. The Sheep Gate is mentioned in Nehemiah 3:1. It was an important gate between the Tower of the Hundred and the upper corner of the Gate of the Guard, different parts of the wall surrounding Jerusalem. Near the Sheep Gate was the sheep market. Sheep shearers are mentioned in Genesis 38:12. Those who were described in Hebrews 11:37 as wearing sheepskins were probably very poor.

(choose a, b, or c)

1. A shepherd is _____ (John 10:11).
   a. lazy   b. good and kind   c. careless

2. Shepherds live or stay _____ (John 10:14).
   a. in a shelter   b. in a house   c. with the sheep

3. A shepherd's voice _____ (John 10:4).
   a. is loud   b. is known to his sheep   c. echos

4. Shepherds are _____.
   a. animal trainers   b. tax collectors   c. keepers of sheep (John 10:14).

5. A good shepherd is _____
   a. dependable   b. loving   c. faithful

6. Who is our Good Shepherd? _____ (John 10:11).
   a. Jesus   b. The Son of God   c. Our Savior

In the underlined words find a letter that is not in the other underlined word. Fill in the blanks with those letters. You'll find some people from our scripture today.

___ In hast but not hat
___ In sheep but not sleep
___ In perk but not park
___ In preach but not reach
___ In hat but not cat
___ In babe but not baby
___ In country but not county
___ In heard but not heart
___ In haste but not hate

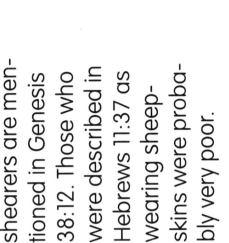

The Bricks of Babel

Skeeter wondered about burning bricks in Genesis 11:3: "let us make bricks, and bake them thoroughly." I tried to explain to my little mouse friend that making bricks was hard work. Clay and straw and some water were used. These ingredients were mixed, sometimes by hand, sometimes by stomping with the feet. Then the mixture was formed into bricks and the bricks were "fired," in a "kiln," or oven. The firing made them hard. Skeeter found it interesting that bricks today are rectangular, as the Israelite slaves of Egypt in early Bible times made them—and were the first to do so. "Good design," Skeeter said. " . . . No, God's design," he added.

As we talked, Skeeter asked me about that big, fiery furnace that Daniel and his friends were in. "Could it be possible—just speculation—" he added, "that it was a big, brick kiln?" I didn't know. But it sure was an interesting thought.

I've left some space for you to draw some rectanglular bricks.

Dictionary definition—stumbling block: a stump or anything that causes one to stumble.

The God of heaven will give us success.
Nehemiah 2:20

Two letters are missing. . . .

S T _ M B L _ N G

COULD ☐ —AND— ☐ BE STUMBLING BLOCKS?

Here is an acrostic about Nehemiah and a beautiful city to be built. Find the answers in Nehemiah 2:1–20.

1. The city where my fathers are buried lies in _____. (v.3)
2. Then I prayed to the God of _____. (v.4)
3. . . . so that I can _____ it. (v.5)
4. (across) "How long will your _____ take..." (v.6) (down) _____ lies in ruins (v. 17)
5. . . . so he will give me _____ to make beams (v.8)
6. The king granted my _____. (v.8)
7. . . . examining the _____ of Jerusalem (v.13)
8. The God of heaven will give us _____. (v.20)

In A Hurry

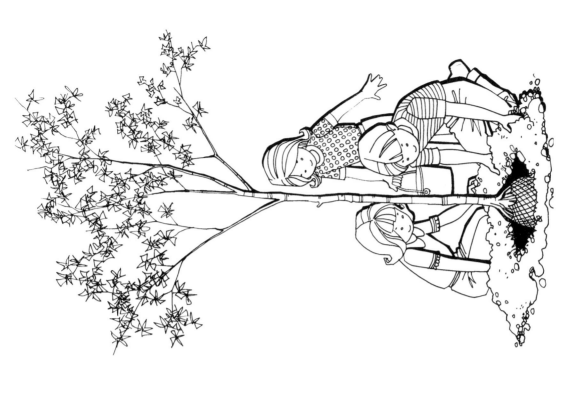

Answers

(1) *Jericho*   (2) *man*   (3) *Zacchaeus*   (4) *wealthy*   (5) *Jesus*
(6) *short*   (7) *sycamore*   (8) *today*

Happy New Year

H – ear God's Word . . . . Isaiah 55:3
A – nswer God's call . . . . Matthew 11:28
P – ardon receive . . . . Nehemiah 9:17
P – eace possess . . . . Romans 15:33
Y – ield to God . . . . Romans 6:13

N – o condemnation . . . . Romans 8:1
E – ternal life is a gift . . . . Romans 6:23
W – alk uprightly . . . . Isaiah 57:2

Y – outh is the time for service . . Ecclesiastes 12:1
E – arly seek God . . . . Psalm 63:1
A – ttend to God's words . . . . Numbers 12:6
R – ejoice in the Lord . . . . Philippians 4:4

Zacchaeus

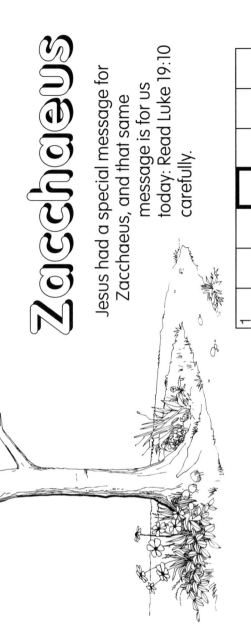

The message today from the Book of Luke, chapter 19:1–10, is a story about Zacchaeus. Answer these questions and write your answers in the squares. You'll find out something about Zacchaeus.

Be sure to listen to the story from God's Word, the Bible.

Jesus had a special message for Zacchaeus, and that same message is for us today: Read Luke 19:10 carefully.

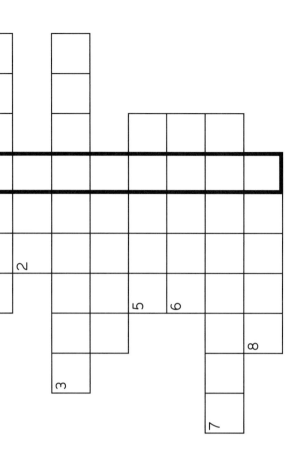

1. To what city does this story take us today? (v.1)
2. A _____ was there. (v.2)
3. What was the man's name? (v.2)
4. Was he poor or wealthy? (v.2)
5. Who was Zacchaeus trying to see? (v.3)
6. Zacchaeus was _____. (v.3)
7. What kind of tree did he climb? (v.4)
8. When was Jesus coming to his house? (v.5)

Children's Bulletin

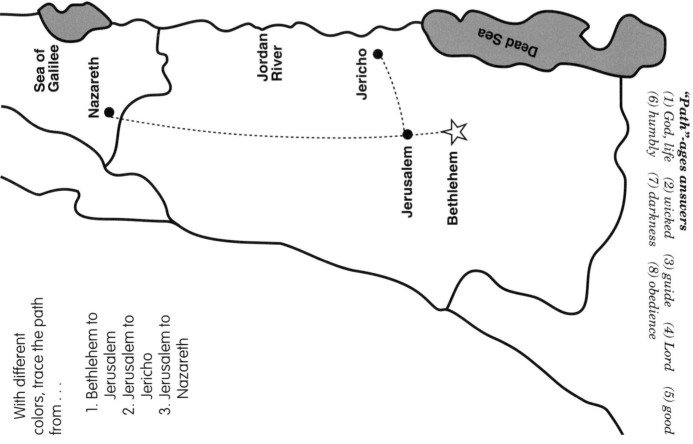

With different colors, trace the path from . . . .

1. Bethlehem to Jerusalem
2. Jerusalem to Jericho
3. Jerusalem to Nazareth

Sea of Galilee

Nazareth

Jordan River

Jericho

Jerusalem

Bethlehem

Dead Sea

"Path"-ages answers
(1) *God, life* (2) *wicked* (3) *guide* (4) *Lord* (5) *good*
(6) *humbly* (7) *darkness* (8) *obedience*

Take a walk through the Bible path... ages.

1. That I may walk before _____ in the light of _____. Psalm 56:13

2. Blessed is the man who does not walk in the counsel of the _____. Psalm 1:1

3. When you walk, they will _____ you. Proverbs 6:22

4. Let us walk in the light of the _____. Isaiah 2:5

5. Ask where the _____ way is, and walk in it. Jeremiah 6:16

6. Walk _____ with your God. Micah 6:8

7. Whoever follows me will never walk in _____. John 8:12

8. That we walk in _____ to his commands. 2 John 1:6

cut out

*ETERNAL TREASURES

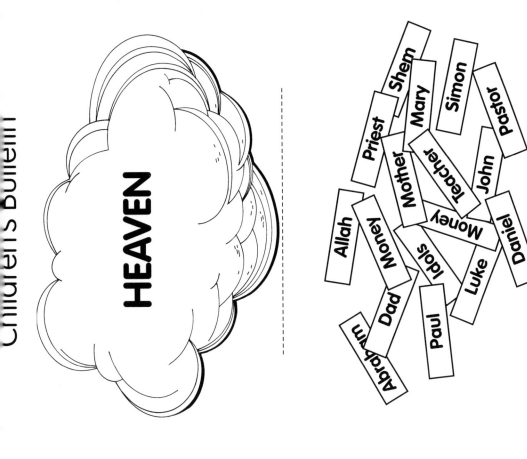

HEAVEN

Shem · Priest · Mary · Simon · Pastor · Allah · Mother · Teacher · John · Money · Idols · Luke · Daniel · Dad · Paul · Abraham

For there is no other name under heaven by which we must be saved. Acts 4:12

Read this from the bottom up.

without Christ.
never go to heaven
But we can

without 10,000 other things
without friends
without beauty
without culture
without big earnings
without learning
without name
without fame
without health
without wealth
We may go to heaven

```
R N A M E U N D E R H E A V
E U A P E T F O R T U N E
H T E L I P O R P R I E S T N
T D A N I E L U K E J A G
O A M R E U M A S H E M I
O D I B O W E R D N A M V
N Z P A D R E P A L O E
S O V O E H T H J O H N
I M S P H Y T R E H I C A E T
E I U W A E M O T H Y O
R S H K R A M R E H T O M
E E E S H E M P I L I H P E
H R J M E N Z I S T E R I C N
T S A V E D A C T S 2 1 4 B
E B T S U M E W H C I H W Y
```

Under Heaven Word Find

Find the following words in the word find:

Starting with I, go up and around for a portion of the verse found in Acts 4:12 and fill in the blanks.

Abraham
Andrew
Daniel
Dad
fortune
idol
Jesus
Luke
John

Mark
minister
money
mother
Padre
Paul
Peter
Philip
prophet

priest
Reba
Matthew
Reverend
Samuel
Shem
Simon
Timothy
teacher

```
R N A M E U N D E R H E A V
E L U A P E T F O R T U N E
H T E H P O R P R I E S T N
T D D A N I E L U K E J A G
O A M R L E U M A S H E M I
O D I B O M W E R D N A M V
N N P A D R E T E P A L O E
S O V O I E H T H J O H N N
I M S P H V T R E H C A E T
E I U W A E T I M O T H Y O
R S S B K R A M R E H T O M
E E E S H E M P I L I H P E
H R J M I N I S T E R I C N
T S A V E D A C T S 4 1 2 B
E B T S U M E W H C I H W Y
```

_____ _____ _____ _____

_____ _____ _____ _____

_____ _____ _____

_____ : _____

2.

Children's Bulletin

Find one answer to a NEW BEGINNING.
With a pencil shade in all the EVEN numbers—2, 4, 6, 8.

9	1	3	5	7	9	1	3	5	7	9	3	5	7	9
1	2	4	6	8	2	4	6	2	4	6	8	2	4	1
3	4	1	3	5	4	7	6	9	8	4	1	8	6	3
5	6	2	4	7	6	9	8	2	6	6	8	3	3	5
7	5	7	6	9	8	1	4	3	4	8	2	7	9	7
9	2	4	8	1	2	3	6	5	2	2	7	8	4	9
1	3	5	7	9	1	3	5	7	9	1	5	9	1	1
3	2	4	3	5	2	4	6	8	3	6	7	9	3	6
5	4	6	5	7	4	6	1	3	6	8	5	7	9	2
7	6	3	4	5	6	4	7	9	8	2	3	5	7	8
9	8	1	2	3	8	2	5	7	9	4	1	6	8	2
1	2	5	7	8	2	8	9	1	3	6	5	4	2	4
3	4	9	1	6	4	6	4	8	6	8	2	3	6	3
5	7	9	1	3	5	7	5	7	9	1	3	1	7	5

Answers
*Fill-in-the-blanks: God created the heavens and the earth; the Word;
beginning; and the Omega.*

BEGINNING . . .

Look up these verses and fill the blanks with the words that are missing.

In the beginning _____ _____ _____. Genesis 1:1

In the beginning was _____ _____. John 1:1

That which was from the _____. 1 John 1:1

I am the Alpha _____. Revelation 1:8 (Alpha means the beginning.)

Did you notice that three of these verses are the first (1st) verse of the first (1st) chapter of these books? The first is a start—a beginning. It ALL starts with God (Genesis 1:1).

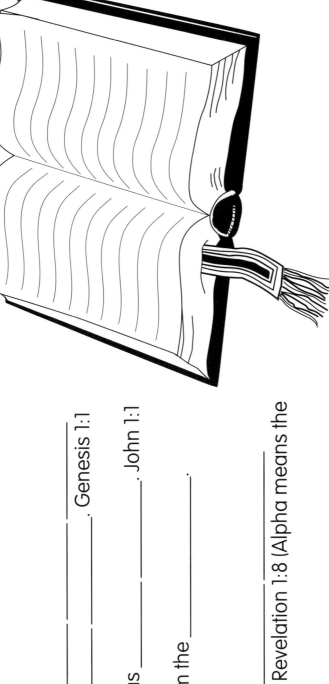

WORTHY IS THE LAMB

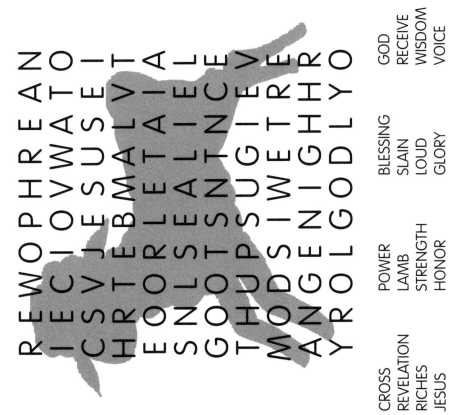

```
R E W O P H R E A N
I E C I O V W A T O
C S V J E S U S E I
H R T E B M A L V T
E O R L E T A I A L
S N L S E A L I E L
G O O T S N T N C E
T H U P S U G I E V
M O D S I W E T R E
A N G E N I G H H R
Y R O L G O D L Y O
```

CROSS   POWER   BLESSING   GOD

REVELATION   LAMB   SLAIN   RECEIVE

RICHES   STRENGTH   LOUD   WISDOM

JESUS   HONOR   GLORY   VOICE

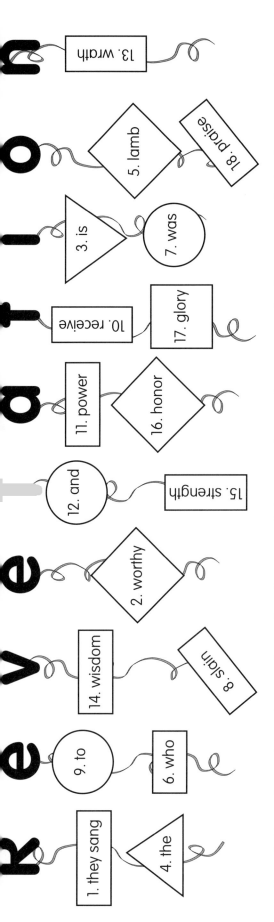

Revelation above has shapes hanging from each letter with numbers in each shape. Match the letter-numbers with the blanks and write the word from the shape into the matching blanks.

Look at the first blank, R–1. Write the words "they sang" on it.

"_____ _____ _____ _____ _____ _____ _____ _____
R–1   E–2   I–3   R-4   O–5   E–6   I–7   V–8   E–9

_____ _____ _____ _____ _____ _____ _____
T–10   A–11   L–12   N–13   V–14   T–17   L–12

_____ _____ _____ _____ _____
L–15   L–12   A–16   L–12   L–12

_____ !"
O–18

Revelation 5:12

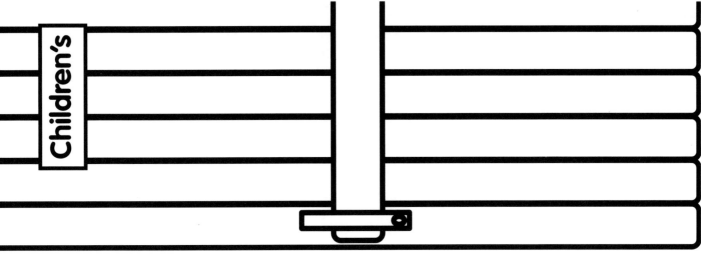

"A Mighty Fortress Is Our God"

is based on Psalm 46.

Find Psalm 46 in your Bible and fill in the blanks.

v. 1 God is our _____ and _____

v. 2 Therefore we will not _____ .

v. 3 though its waters _____ and _____

v. 4 There is a river whose _____ make _____ the city of _____ .

v. 6 _____ are in an _____ kingdoms _____ .

v. 7 The _____ is with us.

v. 9 He makes _____ cease to the ends of the earth.

v. 11 The _____ is with us.

Answers to Psalm 46

(1) refuge, strength   (2) fear   (3) roar, foam   (4) streams, glad, God   (6) Nations, uproar, fall   (7) Lord Almighty   (9) wars (11) Lord Almighty

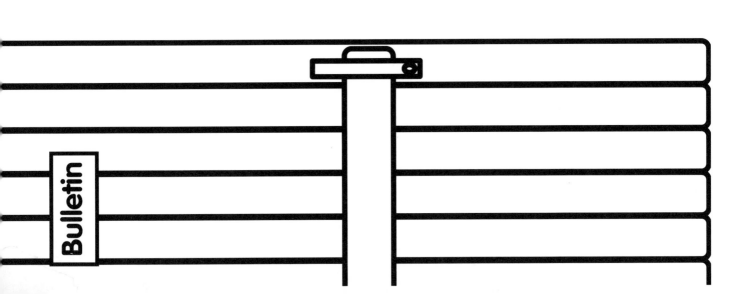

Luther's coat of arms had a circle in it.

The colors in his coat of arms can be found in the word find.

Martin Luther's favorite verse:

"I am . . . the beginning and the ending."
Revelation 1:8 (KJV)

(Like a circle; where does it start? Where does it end?)

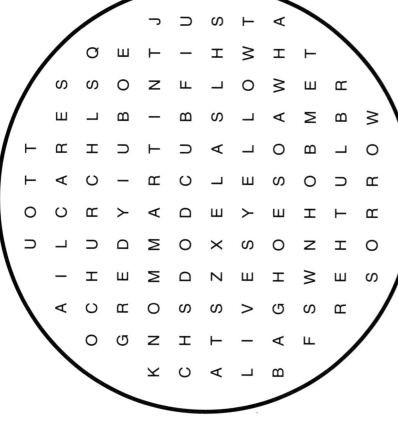

```
      U O T T
  A I L C A R E S
O C H U R C H L S Q
G R E D Y I U B O E
K N O M M A R T I N T J
C H S D O D C U B F I U
A T S Z X E L A S L H S
L I V E S Y E L L O W T
B A G H O E S O A W H A
  F S W N H O B M E T
    R E H T U L B R
      S O R R O W
```

Coat of Arms word find:

Bible	cross	Lamb	sin
black	day	lives	Son
care	faith	Luther	sorrow
church	flower	Martin	white
circle	God	monk	yellow
	just	red	

DIRECTIONS AND PATTERNS
FOR PREPARING BULLETIN COVERS

MONUMENTS
JOSHUA 4:1–9

Materials and tools

glue
broken egg shells (12 pieces
   for each bulletin)

Prepare ahead

Run off bulletins.
Save egg shells, broken in
pieces (brown and white, if
possible).

Procedure

1. Fold bulletins (book fold).
2. To the center of the **M**-logo on the front of the bulletin, glue 12 pieces of egg shells to resemble stones. Set aside to dry.

It may be interesting for you and each of the children of the congregation to have a piece of granite. Call a local monument company. Explain what you are doing and ask for small pieces of granite.

After the service, a couple of children can pass granite pieces out to the other children in the congregation. Should you choose to do this, please add a note in your bulletin explaining the pieces of granite and telling the children there are pieces of granite for them.

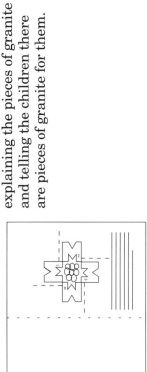

Book Fold

Glue 12 pieces of broken egg shells
to Monument on Front

RAHAB
JOSHUA 2:1–24

Materials and tools

paper   paper punch
white   scotch tape
gray   scissors
or beige   red yarn

Prepare ahead

Run off bulletins on white, gray, or beige paper.

Procedure

1. Fold bulletins in half (book fold).
2. Cut one 5"-length piece of red yarn for each bulletin.
3. With a paper punch, punch through the folded bulletin on the X on the window.
4. Knot one end of the red yarn and lace the other end through the hole.
5. Tape the other end in place 2" below the punched hole on the back of the bulletin.

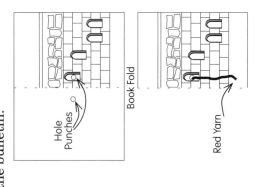

Hole
Punches

Book Fold

Red Yarn

4

POTTER'S VESSEL
JEREMIAH 18:1–12

Materials and tools

yarn
scissors
tapestry needle, size #13
beige/tan color of paper

Prepare ahead

Run off bulletins on a beige/tan color of paper.

Run off tags to be attached.

Procedure

1. Cut out tags.
2. Thread a needle with a piece of the yarn.
3. Poke needle through one shaded dot on the marked earthen vessel. Bring needle out other shaded dot.
4. Lace needle and yarn through top of tag (see next page for pattern). Snip off yarn and tie a knot.
5. Fold bulletins (book fold).

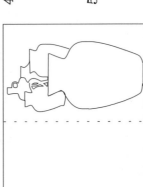

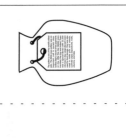

Book Fold

3

BIBLE BITS
JEREMIAH 15:16

Materials and tools

macaroni letters
B, I, T, S
glue

Prepare ahead

Run off the bulletins on brightly colored paper.

Buy alphabet macaroni letters. (Check resources section on how to sort and store.)

Procedure

1. Fold bulletins (book fold).
2. Glue the letters B, I, T, S to the bulletin on the spoon pattern.

Book Fold

Being a potter is one of the world's oldest jobs. The Bible says pottery was an important craft in ancient days. Tax payments from the people were inscribed and baked on clay tablets and kept by scribes. There was a special library with 22,000 volumes in clay. Large pottery jars were used for food storage. In addition to pots and jars, pipes, walls, columns, tubs and nails were made of clay!

Being a potter is one of the world's oldest jobs. The Bible says pottery was an important craft in ancient days. Tax payments from the people were inscribed and baked on clay tablets and kept by scribes. There was a special library with 22,000 volumes in clay. Large pottery jars were used for food storage. In addition to pots and jars, pipes, walls, columns, tubs and nails were made of clay!

Being a potter is one of the world's oldest jobs. The Bible says pottery was an important craft in ancient days. Tax payments from the people were inscribed and baked on clay tablets and kept by scribes. There was a special library with 22,000 volumes in clay. Large pottery jars were used for food storage. In addition to pots and jars, pipes, walls, columns, tubs and nails were made of clay!

Being a potter is one of the world's oldest jobs. The Bible says pottery was an important craft in ancient days. Tax payments from the people were inscribed and baked on clay tablets and kept by scribes. There was a special library with 22,000 volumes in clay. Large pottery jars were used for food storage. In addition to pots and jars, pipes, walls, columns, tubs and nails were made of clay!

Being a potter is one of the world's oldest jobs. The Bible says pottery was an important craft in ancient days. Tax payments from the people were inscribed and baked on clay tablets and kept by scribes. There was a special library with 22,000 volumes in clay. Large pottery jars were used for food storage. In addition to pots and jars, pipes, walls, columns, tubs and nails were made of clay!

Being a potter is one of the world's oldest jobs. The Bible says pottery was an important craft in ancient days. Tax payments from the people were inscribed and baked on clay tablets and kept by scribes. There was a special library with 22,000 volumes in clay. Large pottery jars were used for food storage. In addition to pots and jars, pipes, walls, columns, tubs and nails were made of clay!

6

4-M's
MICAH 4:1–5

Materials and tools

scissors   glue

Optional

tiny reclosable double-stick
plastic bags scotch tape.
M&M candies
(five-six pieces
per bag)

Prepare ahead

Run off bulletins.
Run off scrolls
  to be attached.
Optional
Prepare bags
  of M&M candies.

Procedure

1. Fold bulletins (book fold).
2. Cut out mini scrolls using pattern below.
3. Place scissor blade at arrow,
  on non-printed side of
  scroll. Firmly slide blade
  down to get a curl.
4. Turn paper around and
  repeat step 3.
5. Dab glue in center of *M*-logo
  and attach scroll.
Optional
6. Put a piece of tape inside
  bulletin.
7. Affix plastic bag of M&Ms
  to tape.

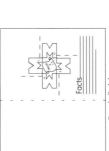   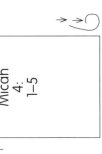

Facts

Book Fold

Micah
4:
1–5

Book Fold

5

PULSE DIET PLAN
DANIEL 1:8–21

(Pulse is an old word for vegetables and grains—possibly
barley, beans, lentils, peas, rye, and wheat.)

Prepare ahead

Run off bulletins
  on white paper.
Run off box pattern on
  brightly colored paper.

Materials and tools

scissors   bright color
glue   of paper

Procedure

1. Fold bulletins (book fold).
2. Cut out mini cereal boxes.
3. Fold on lines and crease all folds well.
4. Bring back of A section over the back of B section and
  lightly glue.
5. Glue mini box onto area marked for box on bulletin cover.
6. Tuck in top and bottom flaps.

B

Pulse*
*Grains from God

10-Day... Pulse Plan

A

Book Fold

PULSE

"Grains from God"

Vitamin C, Calcium, Iron, Phosphorus, Potassium, and all Natural Grains

Barley, Peas, Beans, Lentils, Rye and Beans

10–Day Pulse Plan

A

B

THE GREATEST FISH STORY

LUKE 5:1–11, MATTHEW 4:18–22, OR MARK 1:16–20

Prepare ahead

Run off bulletins
on blue paper.
Prepare bags
of fish crackers.

Materials and tools

scissors
blue paper
small ziplock bags
double-stick scotch tape
fish crackers

Procedure

1. Fold bulletins (place card fold).
2. Put a piece of double-stick tape in the middle of the fish net inside bulletin.
3. Affix a bag of fish crackers to the tape.

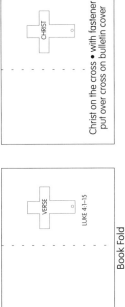

Place Card Fold

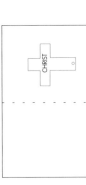

Bulletin Inside

TEMPTATION

LUKE 4: 1–15

Prepare ahead

Run off bulletins on any
color of paper.
Run off cross cut-outs on
white paper.

Materials and tools

colored paper   scissors
1/4", two-pronged
paper fasteners

Procedure

1. Fold bulletins (book fold).
2. Cut out the crosses.
3. Poke a hole in the small circle marked on cross and on bulletin front.
4. Insert two-pronged paper fastener through hole on cross, then into the bulletin. Open the prongs on back of bulletin cover to fasten.

CHRIST

Christ on the cross ● with fastener
put over cross on bulletin cover

VERSE

LUKE 4:1–15

Book Fold

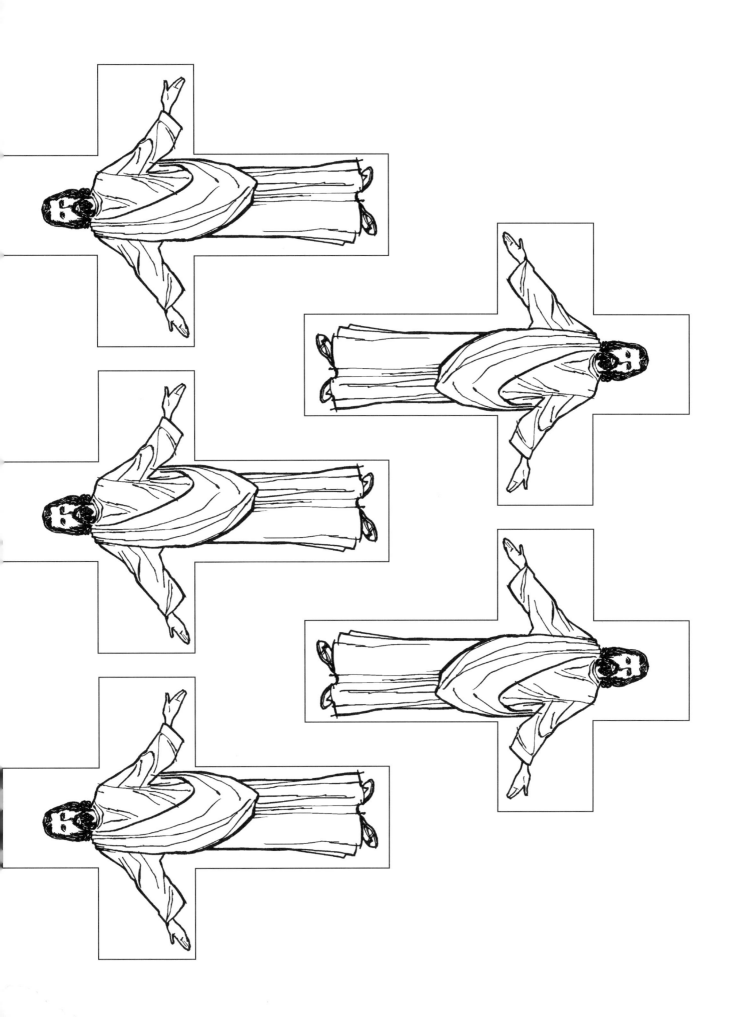

10

MOUSE TRAP
ROMANS 1:18–32

Materials and tools

small yellow
sponge

glue
scissors

Prepare ahead

Run off bulletins.

Procedure

1. Fold bulletins (book fold).
2. Snip off a small piece of the sponge.
3. Glue the piece of sponge to the mouse trap.

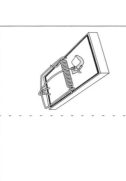

Book Fold

9

BAND-AID WORLD
JOHN 16:33

Materials and tools

double-stick
scotch tape
glue

band-aids
scissors

Prepare ahead

Run off bulletins.
Run off John 16:16a.

Procedure

Inside of bulletin:
1. Cut out printed squares with John 16:16.
2. Glue top edge of squares to "*Glue here*" on bulletin.

Bulletin cover:

1. Fold bulletins (book fold).
2. Fasten band-aid on the world with a small piece of double-stick scotch tape.

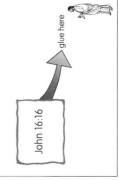

John 16:16

glue here

Bulletin Inside

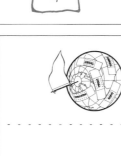

Book Fold

*I*n a little while,
you will see me no more,

*I*n a little while,
you will see me no more,

*I*n a little while,
you will see me no more,

*I*n a little while,
you will see me no more,

12

MYOPIA
1 CORINTHIANS 2:9

Materials and tools

gold cross stickers, 1/2"
brightly colored paper

Prepare ahead

Run off bulletins
on brightly colored paper.

Procedure

1. Fold bulletins (place card fold).
2. Affix a gold cross sticker in the pupil of each eye.

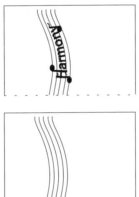

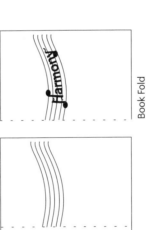

Place Card Fold

11

LIVE IN HARMONY
ROMANS 15:5–6

Materials and tools

scissors
musical stamp and gold or
silver stamp pad; or musical note stickers (colored
metallic notes are avail-
able in packages.)
blue paper

Prepare ahead

Run off bulletins
on blue paper.

Procedure

1. Fold bulletins (book fold).
2. Stamp notes or affix musical note stickers
on music staff on cover.

Book Fold

14

TO SAVE SINNERS
1 TIMOTHY 1:15

Materials and tools

scissors   glue

Prepare ahead

Run off bulletins.
Run off verse.

Procedure

1. Fold bulletins (book fold).
2. Cut out verses.
3. To fold verses, fold down and crease well at the world half. Repeat with other side.
4. Center verse on the cross. Bring the left side of folded world up to the center, fold and crease.
5. Repeat with the right side of the world. It will complete the world picture.
6. Lightly glue in place.

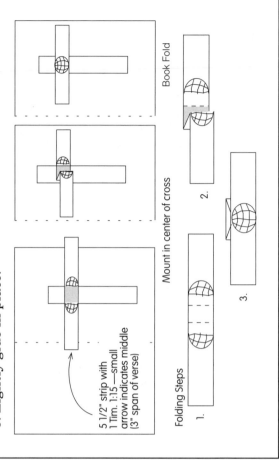

5 1/2" strip with
1 Tim. 1:15—small
arrow indicates middle
(3" span of verse)

Mount in center of cross

Book Fold

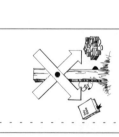

2.

3.

Folding Steps

1.

13

TITHING
1 CORINTHIANS 16:1–2

Materials and tools

two-pronged
paper fasteners, 1/2"
colored paper

Prepare ahead

Run off bulletins.
Run off arrow patterns
on contrasting color
from bulletins.

Procedure

1. Fold bulletins (book fold).
2. Cut out arrows.
3. Poke hole in X's marked on bulletin front and on arrows.
4. Insert paper fastener in Directions arrow and then into "1 Corinthians 16:1–4" arrow. Then insert into bulletin cover. Open prongs to fasten.
5. Adjust the arrows to correctly point the 1 Corinthians arrow to the Bible and the Directions arrow to the money.

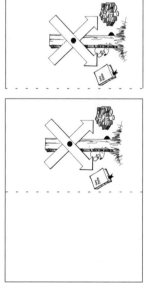

Book Fold

From: **1 Cor** ⊕ **inthians 16:2**

Direc tions: for

From: **1 Cor** ⊕ **inthians 16:2**

Direc tions: for

From: **1 Cor** ⊕ **inthians 16:2**

Direc tions: for

From: **1 Cor** ⊕ **inthians 16:2**

Direc tions: for

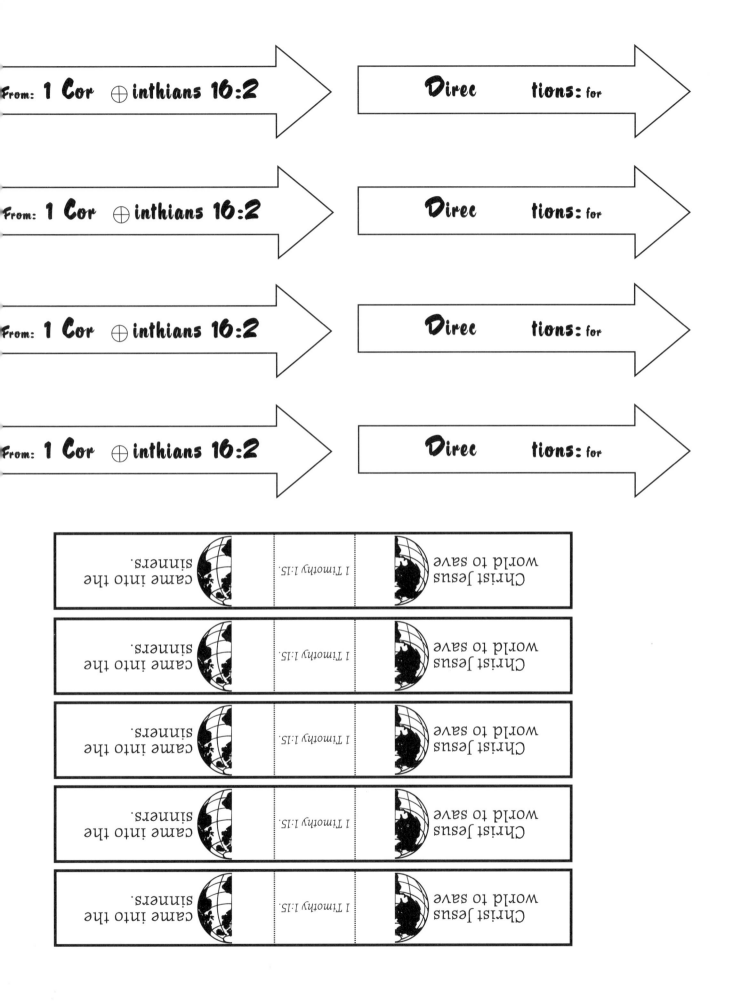

Christ Jesus
world to save
1 Timothy 1:15
came into the
sinners.

Christ Jesus
world to save
1 Timothy 1:15
came into the
sinners.

Christ Jesus
world to save
1 Timothy 1:15
came into the
sinners.

Christ Jesus
world to save
1 Timothy 1:15
came into the
sinners.

Christ Jesus
world to save
1 Timothy 1:15
came into the
sinners.

Prepare ahead

Run off bulletins.
Run off F pattern.
Collect used red, white,
and blue envelopes.

Materials and tools

scissors
red, white, and blue
  envelopes
paper clips

Procedure

1. Fold bulletins (book fold).
2. Cut 2-1/2" corners from red, white, and blue envelopes as shown on diagram.
3. Cut out F's. Cut into pieces on lines. Put in pre-cut envelope corners.
4. Slip envelope corner over bulletin corner and fasten with paper clip. (The envelope corner makes an excellent bookmark!)

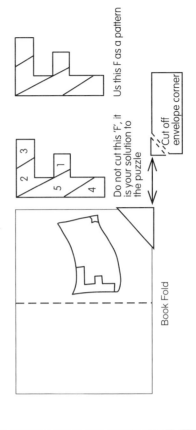

Us this F as a pattern

Do not cut this 'F', it is your solution to the puzzle

Cut off envelope corner

Book Fold

Prepare ahead

Run off bulletins.
Make copies of wrinkled church and spotted church pattern. Run off supply needed for three churches per bulletin.

Materials and tools

stapler
glue
scissors or paper cutter
  (Do not cut more than
  5 sheets at a time.)

Procedure:

1. Fold bulletins (book fold).
2. Cut out churches. For wrinkled church, wad paper up tightly and smooth out lightly.
3. Assemble churches in this order: plain church, spotted church, wrinkled church.
4. Staple the 3 churches together.
5. Glue stapled edge to bulletin front.

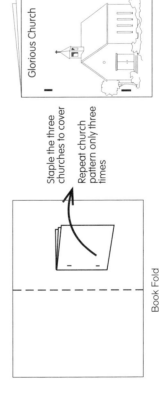

Glorious Church

Staple the three churches to cover

Repeat church pattern only three times

Book Fold

Spotted Church

Children's Bulletin
Wrinkled Church

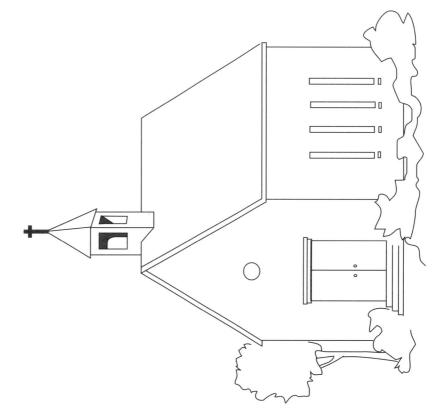

18

SALVATION UMBRELLA

(Adapted from the wordless book by Child Evangelism. Check "resources" for address if you want to include a children's salvation tract.)

Materials and tools

colored paper: green, white, red, black, and yellow
scissors
two-pronged paper fasteners

Prepare ahead

Run off bulletins.
Run off pattern of umbrella ribs on green, white, red, black, and yellow paper, one rib of each color for each bulletin.

Optional: Check Patterns and Ideas section for special envelope for salvation umbrella bulletin.

Procedure

1. Fold bulletins (book fold).
2. Cut out the colored umbrella ribs. Assemble them in this order: green, white, red, black, yellow.
3. Poke hole in circle marked X on round end of ribs.
4. Insert the paper fastener.
5. Poke hole in bulletin cover X. Insert paper fastener with ribs. Open prongs to fasten.

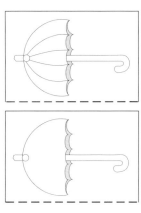

Book Fold   Assemble colors and fasten to umbrella

17

CHRIST'S ASCENSION
REVELATION 3:1–7

Materials and tools

blue paper   scissors
glue   paper clips
2 pieces of Velcro or flocked paper per bulletin

Prepare ahead

Run bulletins off on blue paper.
Run off ascending Christ on white paper.

Procedure

1. Fold bulletins (book fold).
2. Cut out figures.
3. Affix a small piece of velcro or flocked paper to the bulletin on X.
4. Affix the other piece of velcro to the cut out figure.
5. Fasten the figure onto bulletin with a paper clip. Let the children put the figure over the bulletin figure, matching the pieces of velcro.

Book Fold

Put figure of Christ on cover-Velcro will hold.

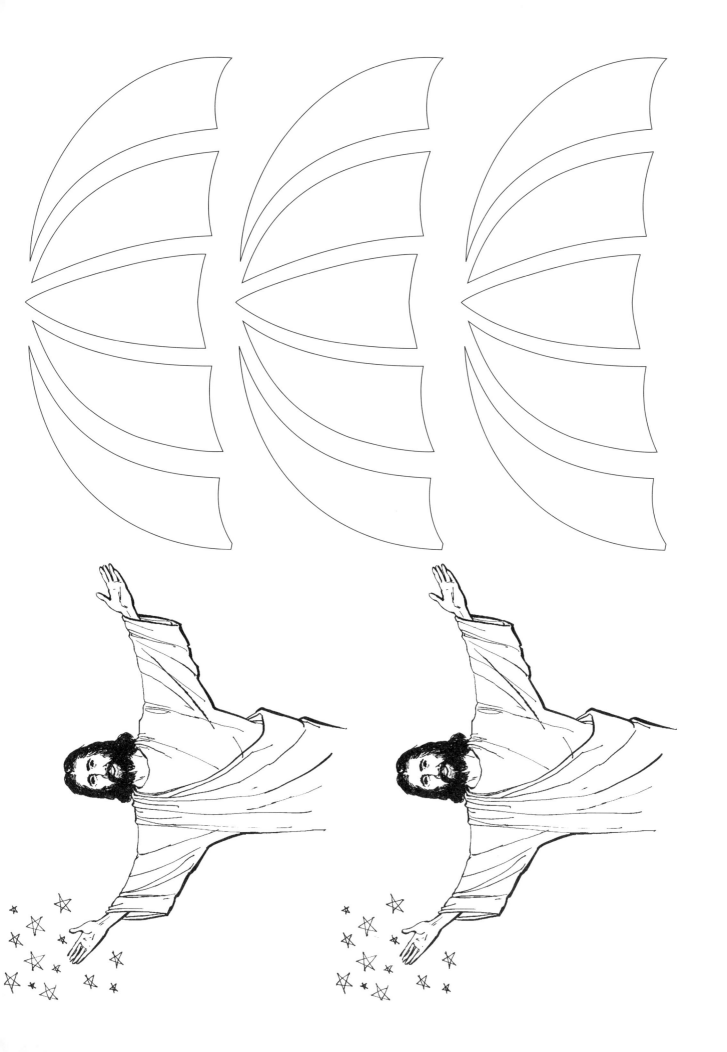

PAUL'S SUITCASE
ROMANS 1:16

Materials and tools

tapestry needle, size #13
paper punch
scissors
yarn

Prepare ahead

Run off bulletins.

Procedure

1. Fold bulletins (place card fold).
2. Cut one 32" length of yarn for each bulletin.
3. Thread piece of yarn in needle.
4. With a needle, poke holes through circles marked on bulletins. Punch through folded bulletin.
5. Open bulletin. With needle, lace through the holes as indicated (Fig. 1). Start from the inside with hole #1. Pull yarn outside, up to #2. Go down #2 and up through #3, leaving slack to allow for the handle. Go down to #4, through #4 and up through #5. Go up to #6, down #6 and up #7, leaving slack for the handle. Poke holes between letters of word find. Come out of #7 and over to #8. Go in #8 and knot the ends with #1.
6. Close bulletin. Slack yarn will be handles. (Fig. 2)

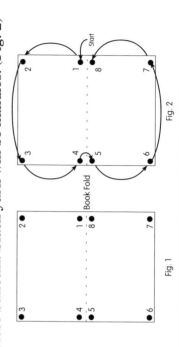

Fig. 1

Fig. 2

Book Fold

Start

REMEMBER OUR MISSIONARIES

Materials and tools

colored paper
colored yarn
scissors

Prepare ahead

Run off bulletins.
Run off world add-on on colored paper.

Procedure

1. Cut out the world add-ons.
2. Punch holes in the marked spots on the bulletin and the world.
3. Attach world to bulletin using about 4" of colored yarn and knotting each end.

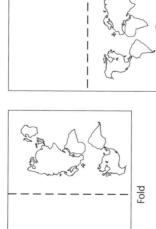

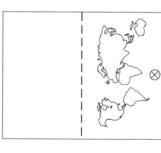

Fold

Place Card Fold

22

WILDERNESS RESTAURANT
EXODUS 16:1–15

Materials and tools

scissors
X-Acto knife and cutting surface
black marker
ruler

Prepare ahead

Run off bulletins.
Run off mini-menus.
With marker and ruler, darken reverse side of diagonal line to match the front.

Procedure

1. Fold bulletins (book fold).
2. Cut out menus.
3. Fold menus on dotted lines as shown in figure so edges meet in middle and darkened edges form an M.
4. Cut slits in front bulletin cover and slip menus in.

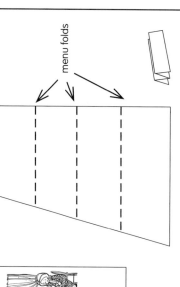

menu folds

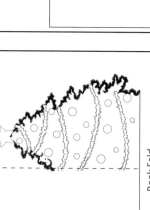

Slit for menu   Book Fold

21

CHRISTMAS TREE
LUKE 2:8–20

Materials and tools

scissors   1" gold star stickers

Optional
glitter   glue
colored yarn   sequins

Prepare ahead

Run off bulletins on green paper.

Procedure

1. Fold bulletins (book fold).
2. Cut carefully around the top and right sides of the tree.
3. Put a gold star at the top of the tree.

Optional

4. Decorate with glitter.

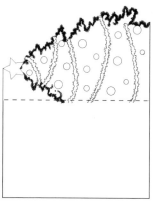

Book Fold

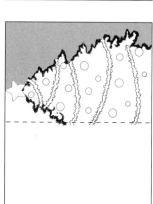

Cut only shaded area around Christmas Tree

24

HOUSE
JOSHUA 24:15

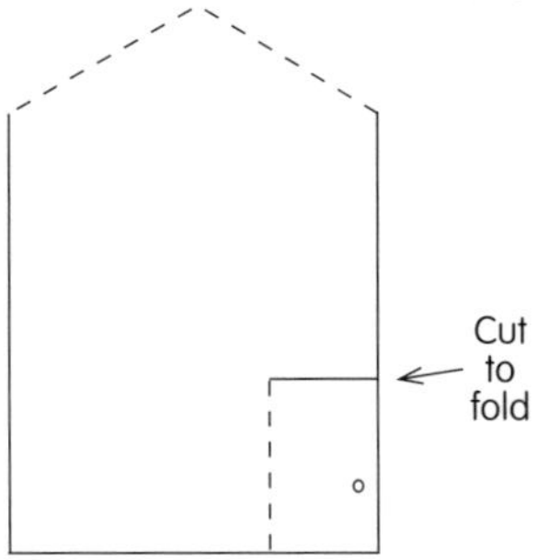

Prepare ahead

Run off bulletins.

Materials and tools

Scissors

Procedure

1. Fold bulletins (book fold). Place folded bulletin face down.

2. Bring A corners down and crease on dotted fold line as shown in figures 1 and 2. Reverse fold and crease well.

3. Bring B corners down and crease well; reverse fold and crease well.

4. Open bulletin.

5. Bring in B's, folding down and in center fold. This will pull bulletin closed. Crease.

6. Fold back page A corner in; fold front page A corner over back page. Crease.

7. Cut door where marked; fold back. Crease.

A

A

A

B

B

B

B

B

A

A

A

Bulletin front and back

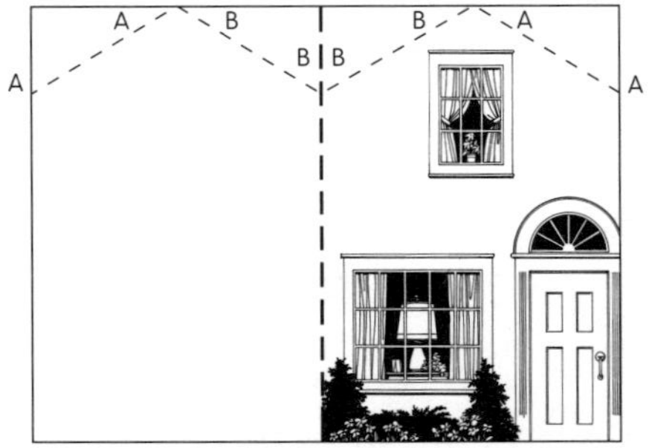

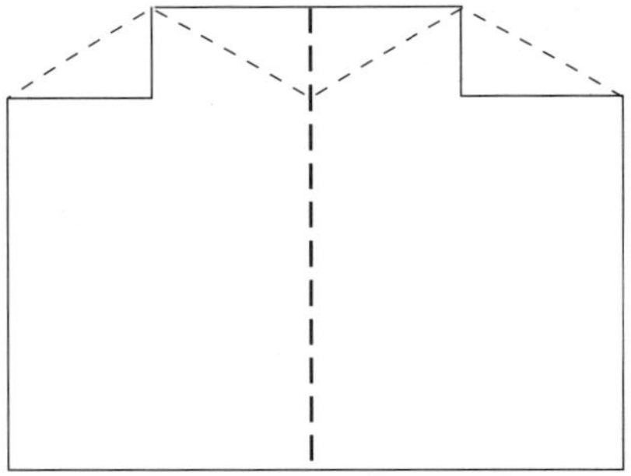

Fig. 1   Book Fold

Bulletin inside pages

Fig. 2

Cut to fold

o

23

PORTABLE CHURCH
EXODUS 35:1–18

Prepare ahead

Run off bulletins.

Materials and tools

five round toothpicks
X-Acto knife
and cutting surface

Procedure

1. Fold bulletins (book fold).
2. Open bulletin, face up.
3. Cut six vertical slits about 1/2 inch apart on vertical lines as indicated.
4. Weave round toothpicks into slits in a staggered pattern

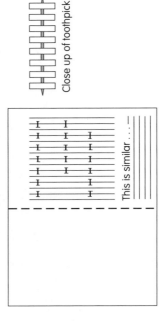

Close up of toothpick

This is similar . . . .

Bulletin front
Weave toothpick in slits

Wilderness Family Menu

All You Can Eat!

Breakfast

Manna*
Fresh Every Morning
The Newest Honey-flavored Wafers.
transported directly from heaven.

Supper

Quail
Fresh and fixed to your liking.

The management asks that you do not take any portions home.

Wilderness Family Menu

All You Can Eat!

Breakfast

Manna*
Fresh Every Morning
The Newest Honey-flavored Wafers.
transported directly from heaven.

Supper

Quail
Fresh and fixed to your liking.

The management asks that you do not take any portions home.

Wilderness Family Menu

All You Can Eat!

Breakfast

Manna*
Fresh Every Morning
The Newest Honey-flavored Wafers.
transported directly from heaven.

Supper

Quail
Fresh and fixed to your liking.

The management asks that you do not take any portions home.

Wilderness Family Menu

All You Can Eat!

Breakfast

Manna*
Fresh Every Morning
The Newest Honey-flavored Wafers.
transported directly from heaven.

Supper

Quail
Fresh and fixed to your liking.

The management asks that you do not take any portions home.

26

EYES OF THE WORLD
2 CHRONICLES 16:9

Prepare ahead

Run off bulletins. Make sure worlds are lined up back to back. Run one to check.
Run off world pattern.

Materials and tools

scissors with small oval handle
scotch tape
old ball-point pen
heavy cardboard
two-pronged paper fasteners 3/4" or 1" in length.

Procedure

1. Cut out eyes of the world. To do so, place bulletin on cardboard, eyes up. Position scissors with one oval handle over an eye. Take an old ball-point pen and firmly move it around inside the handle—twice should do it. Lift up and remove loose piece. Repeat for other eye. (Practice on scrap paper first.)

2. Put a small piece of scotch tape on each side of bulletin over ● spots.

3. Fold bulletins (book fold).

4. Poke holes in the ● spots on the world and bulletin front.

5. Put fastener through holes of world and then bulletin. Open prongs on inside of bulletin.

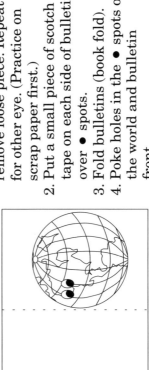

Book Fold

25

CIRCUS TENT
2 SAMUEL 6:1–11

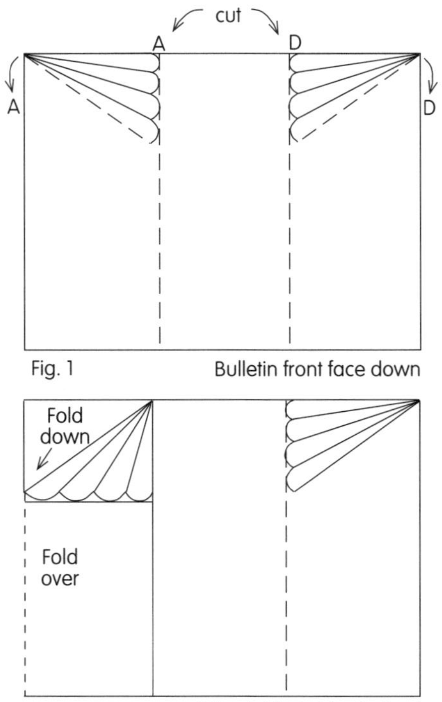

Prepare ahead

Run bulletins off on bright color of paper.

Materials and tools

scissors
bright color of paper

Procedure

1. Fold bulletins (double door fold as shown in Fig. 1). Do not overlap doors. Keep closed.

2. Cut from top along tent edges only. You may cut edges straight or in scallops.

3. Fold the A corner to bulletin front as shown. Crease.

4. Fold the B corner to bulletin front as shown. Crease.

5. Bulletin should look like Fig. 2.

cut

A — D

Bulletin front face down

Fold down

Fold over

Fig. 1

Bring folded sides to front

OT

Fig. 2

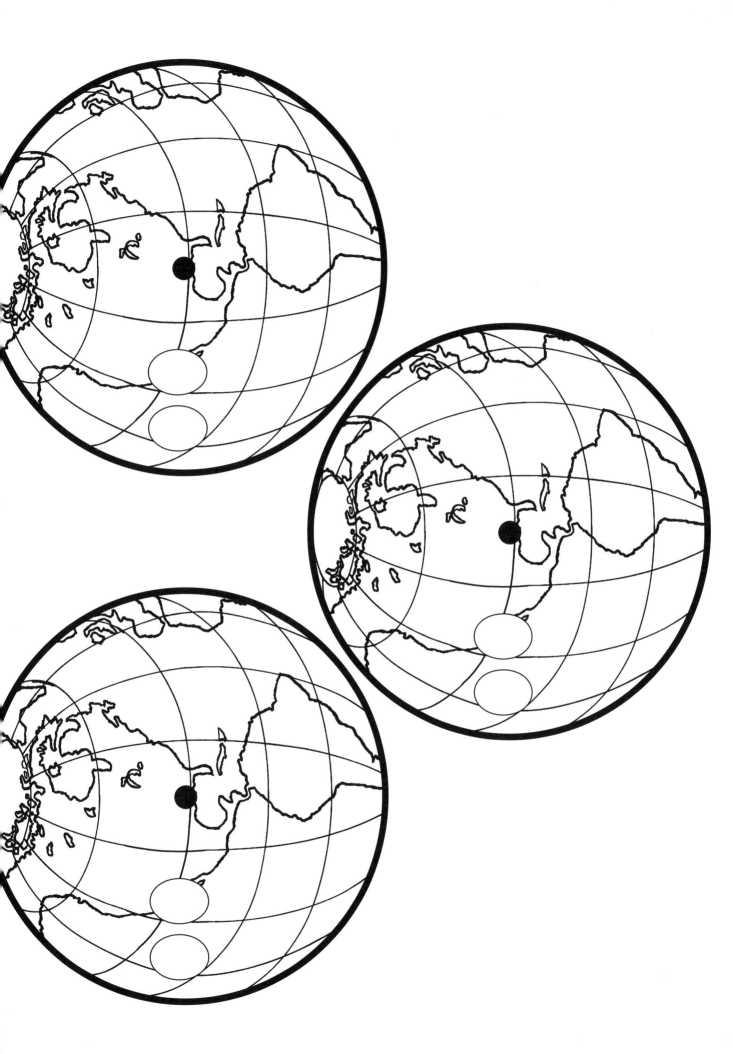

Prepare ahead

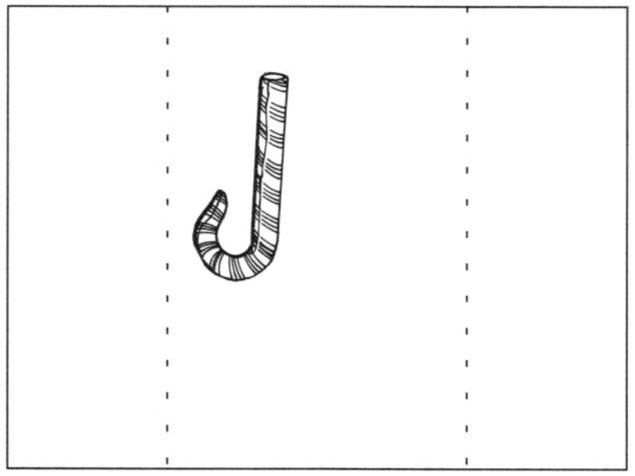

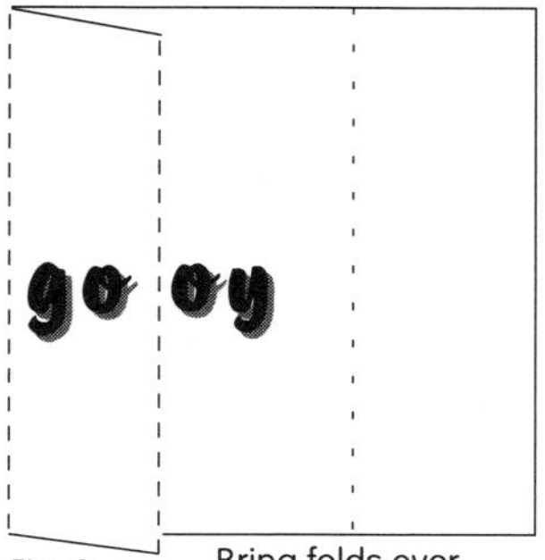

Run off bulletins on green or red paper.

Materials and tools

double-stick scotch tape

small candy canes (2 1/2" or 3" size)

green or red paper

Procedure

1. Lay bulletin with inside facing up. (Fig. 1)
2. Fold both sides over to cover *J* and *Y* only. Do not cover the *O* (Fig. 2). When folded to front, there should be a 1 1/2" space for the inside *O*.
3. Put double-stick tape on the candy cane and place the candy cane upside down on inside of bulletin matching the letter "J".

Inside bulletin

Fig. 1

Bring folds over

Fig. 2

Fig. 3

Optional Plastic Hook

Prepare ahead

Run off bulletins on a neutral shade of paper.

Materials and tools

scissors

neutral shade of paper

two-pronged paper fastener, 1/2" in length

one plastic hook

Procedure

1. Fold bulletins (book fold).
2. Lay bulletin open, inside facing up.
3. Cut heavy line as indicated, 3" down center fold.
4. Fold corner A to inside of bulletin along fold line. Crease well.
5. Fold corner B to inside of bulletin along fold line. Crease well.
6. Poke hole in bulletin front where marked.
7. Put paper fastener through the hole. Slip plastic hook on fastener so the hook is inside the bulletin. Open prongs of fastener and slip under corners A and B.
8. Close bulletin.

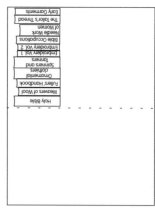

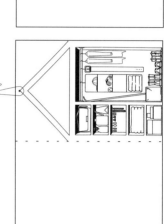

Materials and tools

X-Acto knife and cutting
surface
animal stickers
neutral shade of paper

Prepare ahead

Run off bulletins on a neutral shade of paper.

Procedure

1. Lay bulletin on cutting surface with cover facing up.
2. With X-Acto knife cut sides and top of door of ark.
3. Fold bulletins (place card fold).
4. Put an animal sticker on the inside of the bulletin on spot shown. When door opens, animal can be seen. Use a variety of animal stickers for the bulletins.

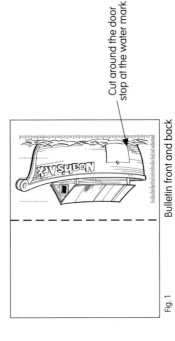

Cut around the door
stop at the water mark

Bulletin front and back

Fig. 1

Materials and tools

X-Acto knife
and cutting surface
scissors
red paper

Prepare ahead

Run off bulletins on red paper.

Put a bell border around bulletin. Ask children how many picture and word bells they can find.

Procedure

1. Lay bulletin open, inside facing down, on cutting surface.
2. With X-Acto knife, cut around the edges of the bell. Stop cutting at arrows as shown in figure. Do not cut the bow or the bottom of the bell. (Once you have a sizeable slit cut you can finish cutting the bell with scissors.)
3. Carefully fold on dotted lines. Crease well.
4. Carefully flip bell with folds.

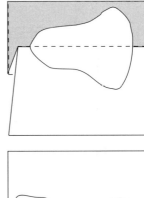

Stop
cutting
at
arrows

Finished Bulletin

Bell will move when
bulletin is opened
and closed carefully.

32

PROVERBS PHARMACY
PROVERBS 2:10–11

This shape can be used with a number of passages from Proverbs.

Materials and tools

scissors

Optional

tiny reclosable bags

small candy (jelly beans)

double-stick scotch tape

Prepare ahead

Run off bulletins.

Procedure

1. Fold bulletins (book fold).
2. Cut away the marked areas.
Optional:
Put candy in bags.
With tape, stick the bag of candy onto the bulletin.

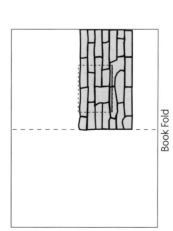

Book Fold

31

JERICHO WALL
JOSHUA 6:1–20

Materials and tools

X-Acto knife and cutting surface

Prepare ahead

Run off bulletins.

Procedure

1. Fold bulletins (book fold).
2. Lay bulletin on cutting surface, inside facing up. With X-Acto knife cut the two sides and top of brick wall as shown.
3. Fold wall down to inside along fold line. Crease and return to standing position.

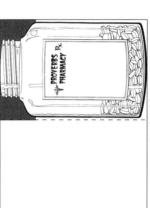

Book Fold

34

THANKSGIVING THEME
LUKE 7:36–50

Prepare ahead

Run off center sheet.

Materials and tools

scissors   glue
stapler
black construction paper
yellow construction paper
white construction paper

Procedure

1. Cut out pattern for pilgrim hat, band, and buckle.
2. Fold sheet of black construction paper (book fold). Place pattern on fold. Trace around pattern and cut out hat.
3. Cut hat band out of white construction paper. Lightly glue white band on hat.
4. Cut buckle out of yellow construction paper. Lightly glue buckle on hat band. Let dry.
5. When dry, fold carefully (book fold.)
6. Fold insert as shown in illustration (double door fold; to fit inside hat when folded).
7. Staple folded insert to the bulletin cover (hat) at center fold.

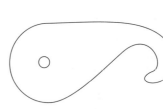

Book Fold

33

FISHERS OF MEN
MATTHEW 17:27 OR LUKE 6:13–14

Prepare ahead

Run off bulletins.

Materials and tools

scissors
Optional
plastic hook
thread
(See bulletin #28 for hook size, etc. Use paper hook if preferred)

Procedure

1. Fold bulletins (place card fold).
2. Cut bottom edge of fish along heavy line. *Optional*
3. Put thread through hole in hook. Knot it and tape hook by fish's mouth.

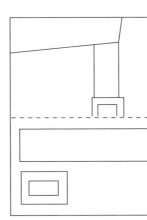

Place Card Fold

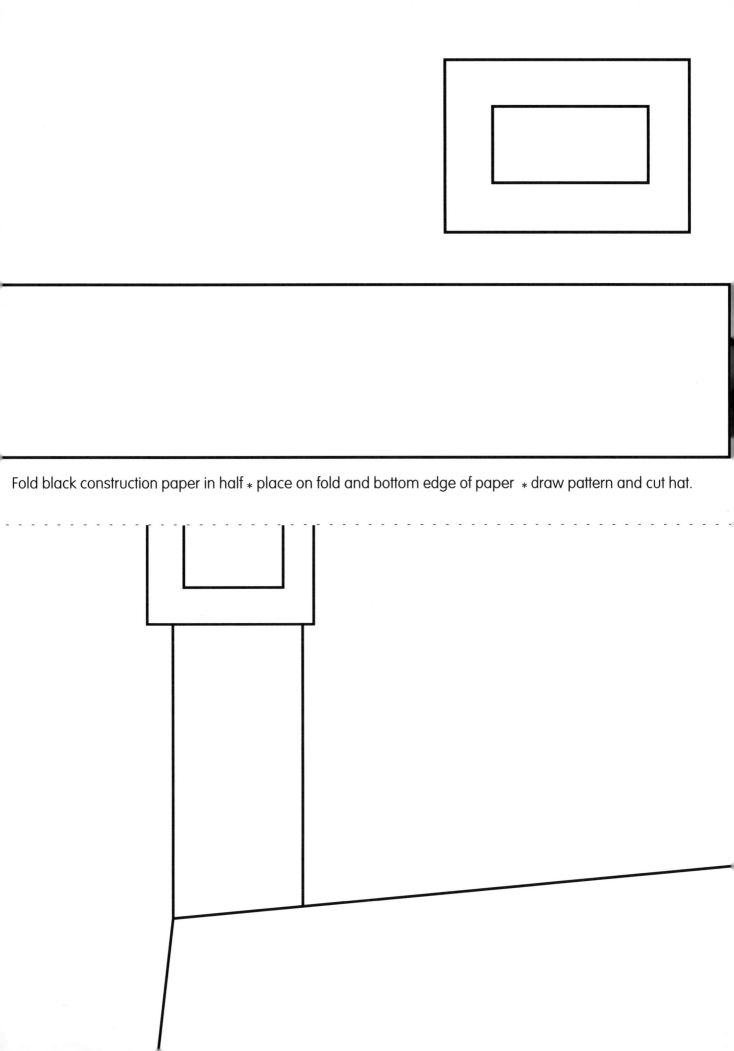

Fold black construction paper in half * place on fold and bottom edge of paper * draw pattern and cut hat.

36

APOKALUPSIS*
REVELATION 2:1–18

Materials and tools

colored paper
scissors
Optional
glue

Prepare ahead

Run off bulletins.
Optional
Run off curtain portion
separately on contrasting
color.

Procedure

1. Cut away the non-curtain portion of cover.
2. Fold bulletins (book fold).
Optional
1. Cut out separate curtain
2. Glue left edge to left edge of bulletin.

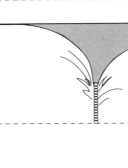
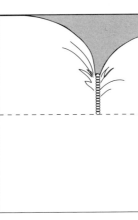

Book fold

35

BUTTERFLY EASTER
JOHN 20:29

Instructions are given for both
a booklet style and a place
card fold bulletin.

Prepare ahead

Run off bulletins front and
back on lavender or purple
paper.
(Be sure picture of Jesus
backs butterfly and bul-
letin text backs text.)

Materials and tools

lavender or purple paper
scissors
Booklet style
stapler

Procedure

Booklet style
1. Cut sheets in half, crosswise.
2. Cut around right side of butterfly wings, leaving left side
solid for stapling.
3. Assemble butterfly cover and back page; staple on left side.

Place card fold
1. Fold bulletins (place card
fold).
2. Cut around sides and bottom of butterfly, leaving
top fold intact.

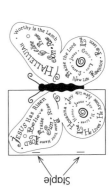

Place Card Fold

staple

MOUSIE HEART
MULTIPLE VERSES

Materials and tools

red paper
scissors
tiny red heart stickers

Prepare ahead

Run off bulletins on red paper.

Procedure

1. Fold bulletins (place card fold). Put red stickers in eyes.

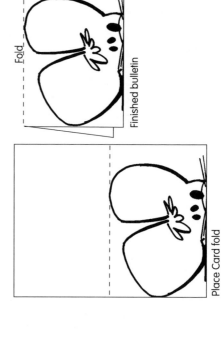

Finished bulletin

Place Card fold

PIGGY BANK
MULTIPLE VERSES

Materials and tools

X-Acto knife and cutting surface
bright pink paper

Prepare ahead

Run off bulletins on light pink paper.
Run off checks on bright green paper and cut apart or send for tract OR gospel money to insert (see "Resources").

Procedure

1. With X-Acto knife cut a slit in piggy bank slot for tract to slip into.
2. Fold bulletins (book fold).
3. Insert tract or gospel money.

Gospel money or tract

Inside bulletin

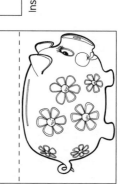

Place Card Fold

TRIM A CHRISTMAS TREE
LUKE 2:1–7

Prepare ahead

Run off bulletins on green paper.

Materials and tools

scissors
green paper
gold star stickers, 1/2" size
multi-colored glitter or sequins
glue

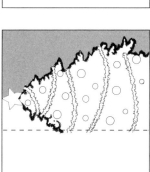

Procedure

1. Fold bulletins (book fold).
2. Cut along heavy outside line of tree and around star.
3. Affix gold star to top of tree.
4. Put a few light dabs of glue here and there.
5. Sprinkle a little glitter over glue. Let dry. Shake off excess and reuse.

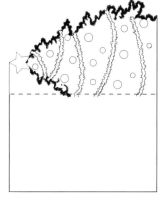

Cut only shaded area around Christmas Tree

SNOWMAN
MULTIPLE VERSES

Prepare ahead

Run off bulletins on white paper.
Run off small snowman insert on white paper.
Run off forts on white paper.

Materials and tools

scissors
X-Acto knife and cutting surface
glue
Optional
white glitter

Procedure

1. Fold bulletins (book fold).
2. Cut away cover back-ground from snowman as shown.

Procedure for insert

1. Cut out small snowman and snow fort around the heavy lines. (Do not cut heavy lines.)
Optional
2. Lightly spread glue here and there on the snow-man and sprinkle with white glitter. Let dry.
3. With X-Acto knife, cut slit into fort where marked.
4. Glue lightly around edges of fort.
5. Slip small snowman into the fort slit.

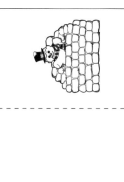

Cut only shaded area around snowman

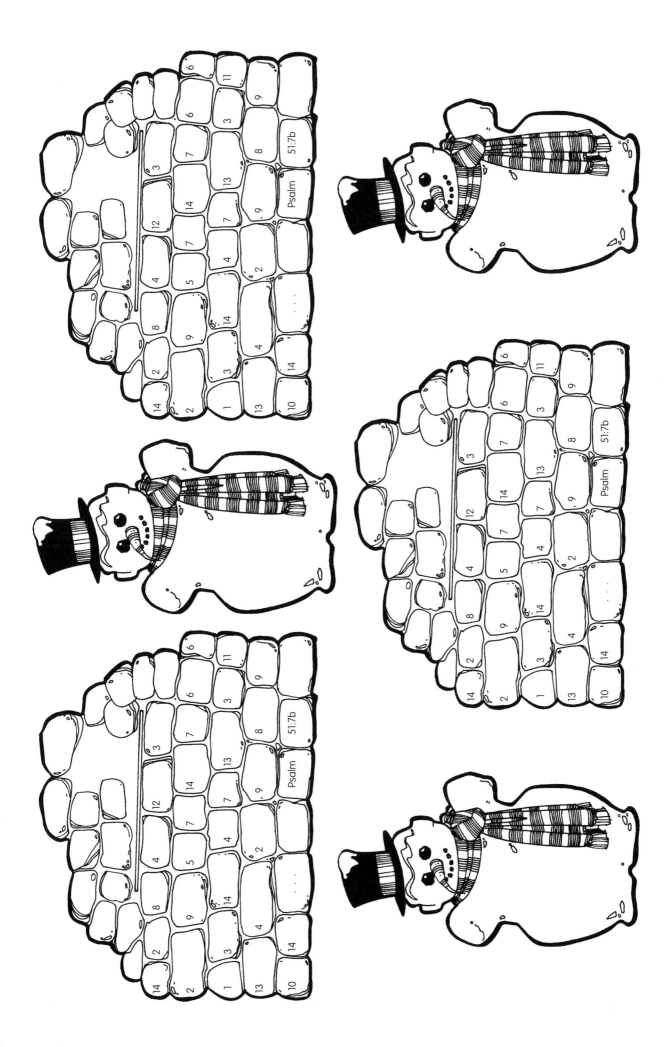

No. John 3:16   Date: Today

The Bank of Eternal Life

Pay to the Order of __Whoever Believes in Me__ $ Priceless

The Sum of __Eternal Life__

Jesus Christ

No. John 3:16   Date: Today

The Bank of Eternal Life

Pay to the Order of __Whoever Believes in Me__ $ Priceless

The Sum of __Eternal Life__

Jesus Christ

No. John 3:16   Date: Today

The Bank of Eternal Life

Pay to the Order of __Whoever Believes in Me__ $ Priceless

The Sum of __Eternal Life__

Jesus Christ

No. John 3:16   Date: Today

The Bank of Eternal Life

Pay to the Order of __Whoever Believes in Me__ $ Priceless

The Sum of __Eternal Life__

Jesus Christ

No. John 3:16   Date: Today

The Bank of Eternal Life

Pay to the Order of __Whoever Believes in Me__ $ Priceless

The Sum of __Eternal Life__

Jesus Christ

No. John 3:16   Date: Today

The Bank of Eternal Life

Pay to the Order of __Whoever Believes in Me__ $ Priceless

The Sum of __Eternal Life__

Jesus Christ

42

Sin in the Camp
Joshua 7:1–21

Materials and tools

X-Acto knife and cutting surface

silver or gold glitter

Prepare ahead

Run off bulletins. Make sure Achan's gold will be aligned with bottom of <u>A</u> on cover when folded.

Procedure

1. Fold bulletins (book fold).
2. Open bulletin.
3. With X-Acto knife, cut the heavy lines on bottom and sides (almost to top) of A on cover.
4. On inside, put a dab of glue under Achan's tent. Sprinkle glitter on glue for stolen treasure.

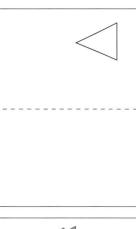

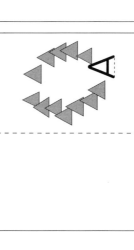

Cut on heavy line, fold down

41

Zipper
Multiple Verses

Materials and tools

Scissors

Prepare ahead

Run off bulletins.

Optional

Scripture text or bulletin name / date may be added to pocket

Procedure

1. Fold bulletins (double door fold).
2. Cut off right and left upper corners along open zipper line.

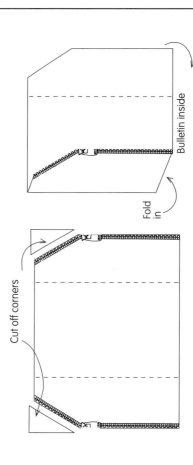

Cut off corners

Fold in

Bulletin inside

44

BROKEN WORLDS
NEHEMIAH 2:4–20

Materials and tools

old ball-point pen
paper clips
small-handled scissors with
oval handle
cardboard for work area

Prepare ahead

Run off bulletins.
Run off inserts, half-page
size (one side brick wall,
the other side broken wall)

Procedure

1. Fold bulletins (place card fold).
2. Open bulletin. Place area to be cut on heavy cardboard.
   Hold scissors handle firmly over eyes on cover. Press ball-
   point pen firmly around the inside of the handle (go
   around twice). The paper should be cut loose; just lift and
   remove! (Practice on scrap paper first.)

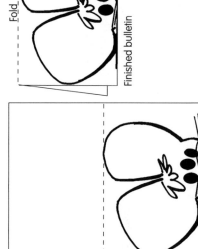

Place Card fold

Fold

Finished bulletin

43

SHEPHERD'S BULLETIN
PSALM 23

Materials and tools

X-Acto knife and cutting
surface
neutral color paper

Prepare ahead

Run off bulletin on a neutral color paper such as
creme or light tan.

Procedure

1. Bulletin cover facing up, use X-Acto knife to cut upper
   arch, right side, and bottom of door. The left side will
   serve as a hinge. Leave stone door frame intact.
2. Fold bulletins (book fold).

Book Fold

In this rebuilt wall, put a word in each brick that would help us to be better Christians.

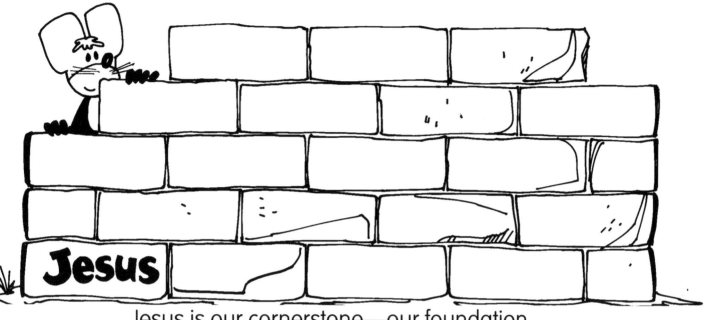

Jesus is our cornerstone—our foundation.

Through Skeeter's eyes, we see a broken brick wall. What a mess! It can be cleaned up and rebuilt. Turn the page over and look again through Skeeter's eyes.

IN A HURRY

LUKE 19: 1–10; FOR NEW YEAR'S

Prepare ahead

Run off bulletins on any color of paper.

Run off the insert folding strip on matching color of paper.

Run off pop-up picture on contrasting color of paper.

New Year's Option

For bulletin back, print extra large outline numbers for the new year (1996).

Here are ideas for inside each number:

#1—Print church name or children's bulletin name.

#9—Print birthday wishes and names.

#9—List helpers and thank them.

#?—Print "Pray for," and list those in need.

Materials and tools

contrasting color of paper

scissors

glue

Procedure

1. Cut out folding strip.
2. Fold in half (follow diagram).
3. Take folded end and bring down to paper edge. Crease on fold lines.
4. Fold forward and backward on each fold.
5. Fold bulletins (book fold).
6. Open bulletin and lay flat, inside facing up. Open strip and place strip 1" from the bulletin top. Align center fold of bulletin to center fold of strip. Be sure diagonal folds of strip point downward. Glue the outside end of each strip to the bulletin. Let dry.
7. Put a small dab of glue on the X (left triangle of strip) and affix your pop-up picture to it.
8. When dry, open and close the bulletin to pop up the picture.

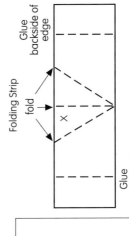

Folding Strip

fold

X

Glue backside of edge

Glue backside of edge

Glue backside of edge

Inside Bulletin

Happy New Year

Glue strip in place
Glue New Year to X

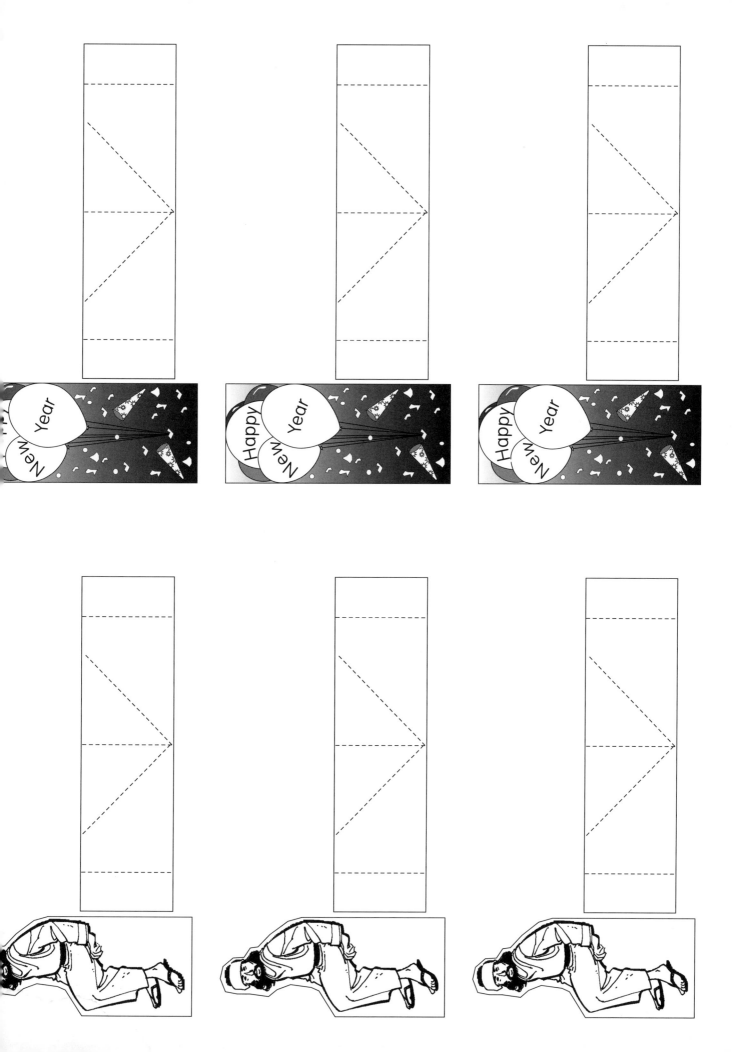

* ETERNAL TREASURE

Prepare ahead

Run off outside bulletins on any color of paper.

Run off inside sheet on white paper. Note that question: Do you know about ET? must be positioned exactly on reverse side of inside bulletin so when flap on outside bulletin is cut and folded printing will appear.

Materials and tools

colored paper
white paper
X-Acto knife and cutting surface
scissors
glue

Procedure

1. Fold cover (book fold).
2. Place cover face up on cutting surface. With X-Acto knife, cut along dotted lines. Fold up on fold line.
3. Fold white bulletin (book fold) and crease well. Reverse fold and crease well. (Folding and creasing is very important.)
4. Lay the inside bulletin face down. Bring up bottom left corner of page toward center fold. Stop when you see the outside edge of the top of the T. Press a fold on that edge of the T and along the diagonal fold line shown in diagram, to center fold. Flip paper over and reverse the fold. Repeat on other side for E. Be sure your first crease is accurate.
5. Lay inside bulletin face up on cutting surface. With X-Acto knife, cut out between the E and T.
6. Cut a slit over E and T.
7. Bring letters inside and crease. Close white bulletin; open to see the ET pop up. (Creasing folds each way will make it open and close smoothly.)
8. Lightly glue the outer edges only of the back of the inside bulletin and affix to the back of the colored bulletin cover. Let dry.

Children's
Bulletin

fold

cut

Front Cover, Outside bulletin

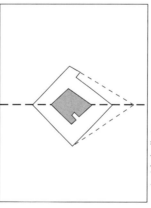

Inside bulletin

Do you
know
about
ET?

Reverse side of inside bulletin

Do You
know
about . . . .
E T * ?

open your bulletin
for the original ET*

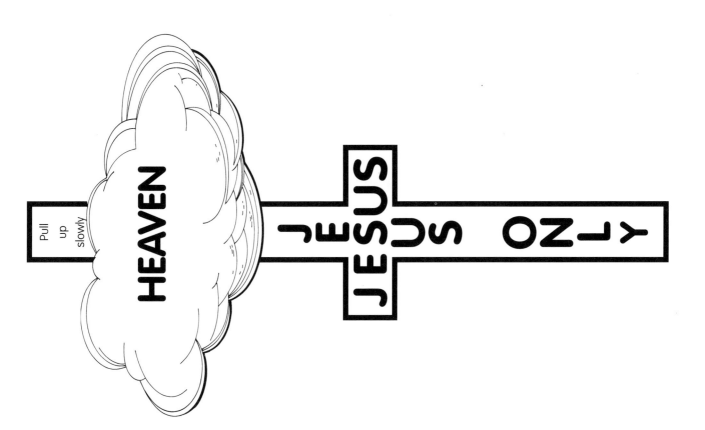

Pull
up
slowly

HEAVEN

JESUS

ONLY

47

NO NAME UNDER HEAVEN
ACTS 4:12

Prepare ahead

Run off bulletins on bright blue paper.

Run off cloud-cross on white paper.

Materials and tools

bright blue paper
white paper
scissors
X-Acto knife and cutting
surface

Procedure

1. Fold bulletins (book fold)
2. Open bulletin. Cut slit with X-Acto knife, reinforce with scotch tape.
3. Cut out cloud-crosses.
4. Slip the cloud-cross into slit. Line up cloud with cloud on bulletin front.
5. Make sure the slit has been cut wide enough for the cross to move in and out smoothly.

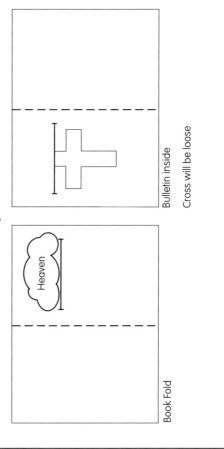

Bulletin inside

Cross will be loose

Book Fold

Heaven

48

NEW BEGINNINGS
2 CORINTHIANS 5:17

Prepare ahead

Run off bulletins (choose color for the season) Run off strip on white paper.

Materials and tools

paper in seasonal color
X-Acto knife and cutting surface
scotch tape, 1/2" wide
paper cutter or scissors

Procedure

1. Fold bulletins (book fold).
2. Open bulletin. Put a 2 1/4" piece of 1/2" scotch tape lengthwise over vertical line on left side of bulletin so line is in middle of tape. Tape will help prevent tearing.
3. With bulletin open, use X-Acto knife to cut slit as indicated on left side of bulletin.
4. Cut strips with scissors or paper cutter. (When using a paper cutter, for clear, sharp cuts, do not cut more than five sheets at a time.)
5. Lay strip with side printed A NEW BEGINNING facing up inside bulletin.
6. Fasten right end of the strip with glue or tape onto edge of right vertical line of bulletin. (Tape will make it lie smoother.)
7. Slip other end of strip through the slit that has been reinforced with scotch tape.
8. Close bulletin, folding inside strip. DO NOT CREASE STRIP.
9. Keeping bulletin closed, slowly pull strip out and read verse.
10. Now slowly open bulletin. Verse will retract inside.

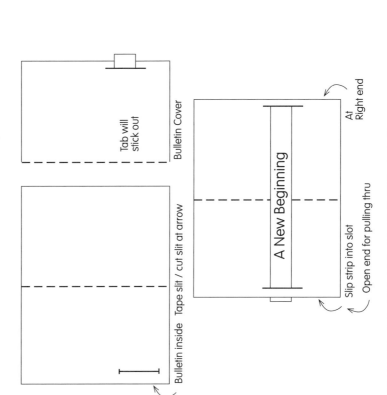

Tab will stick out

Bulletin Cover

Bulletin inside   Tape slit / cut slit at arrow

A New Beginning

At Right end

Slip strip into slot
Open end for pulling thru

A NEW BEGINNING

A NEW BEGINNING

A NEW BEGINNING

The old has gone, the new has come! 2 Corinthians 5:17

The old has gone, the new has come! 2 Corinthians 5:17

The old has gone, the new has come! 2 Corinthians 5:17

49

WORTHY IS THE LAMB
REVELATION 5:11–12

Prepare ahead

Run off bulletins on lavender or purple paper.

Run off the cross on white paper.

Run off the cloud on the same color paper as the bulletin.

Materials and tools

lavender or purple paper

scissors

glue

Procedure

1. Fold bulletins (book fold).

2. Cut out crosses and clouds.

3. Fold cross (follow diagram): #1 is base square. Fold and crease both ways.

4. Crease and fold #2 face to face with #1. Fold under so that #3 is facing up over #2.

5. Crease and fold #5 over #3.

6. Crease and fold #4 over back of #5.

7. Fold and crease #6 down over back of #4.

8. Put a dab of glue on the cloud and affix to the back of #6. Let dry.

9. Put a little glue under #1 and affix to bulletin on the X between the *R* and the *H*.

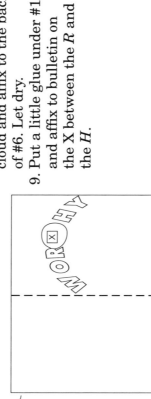

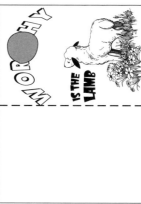

tombstone

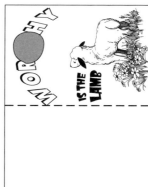

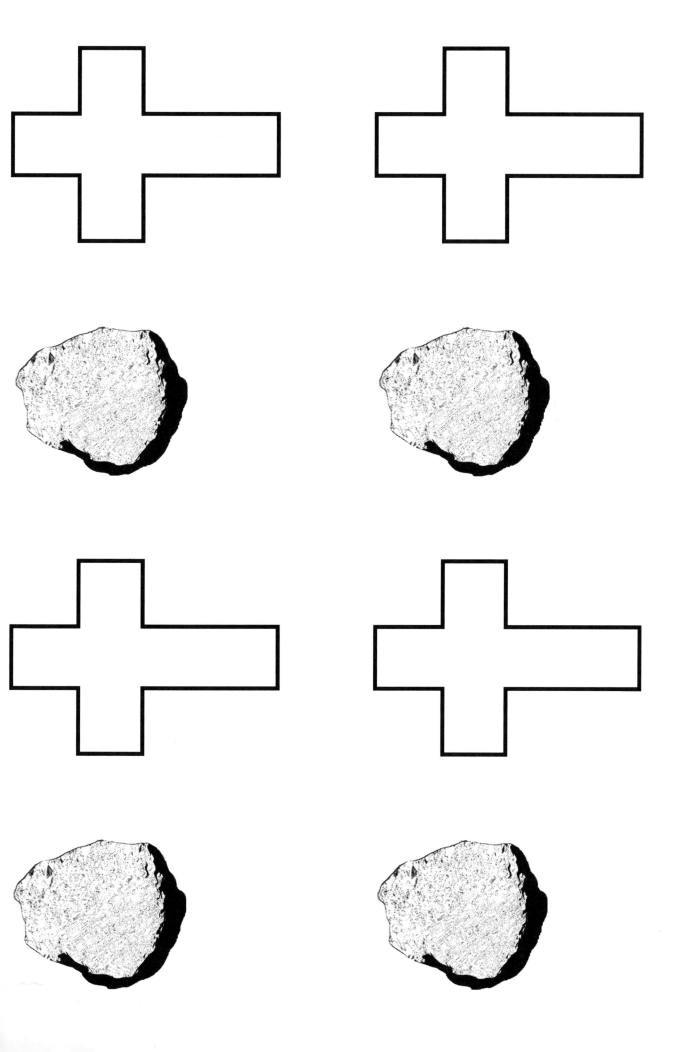

The **Just** shall live by *faith*

The **Just** shall live by *faith*

The **Just** shall live by *faith*

The **Just** shall live by *faith*

The **Just** shall live by *faith*

The **Just** shall live by *faith*

The **Just** shall live by *faith*

The **Just** shall live by *faith*

The **Just** shall live by *faith*

The **Just** shall live by *faith*

The **Just** shall live by *faith*

The **Just** shall live by *faith*

50

MARTIN LUTHER'S THESIS

HEBREWS 10:38

Prepare ahead

Run off bulletins on beige/tan paper.
Run off verse on white paper.

Materials and tools

beige/tan paper
glue
scissors

Procedure

1. Cut out the verses.
2. Fold bulletins (double door fold).
3. Glue verse on the spot marked with an X. The verse will overlap the other door.

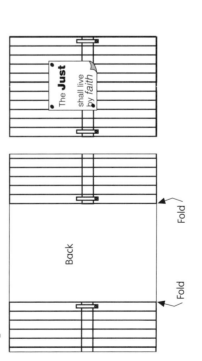

December

November

Happy Birthday

FAITH

JESUS

START

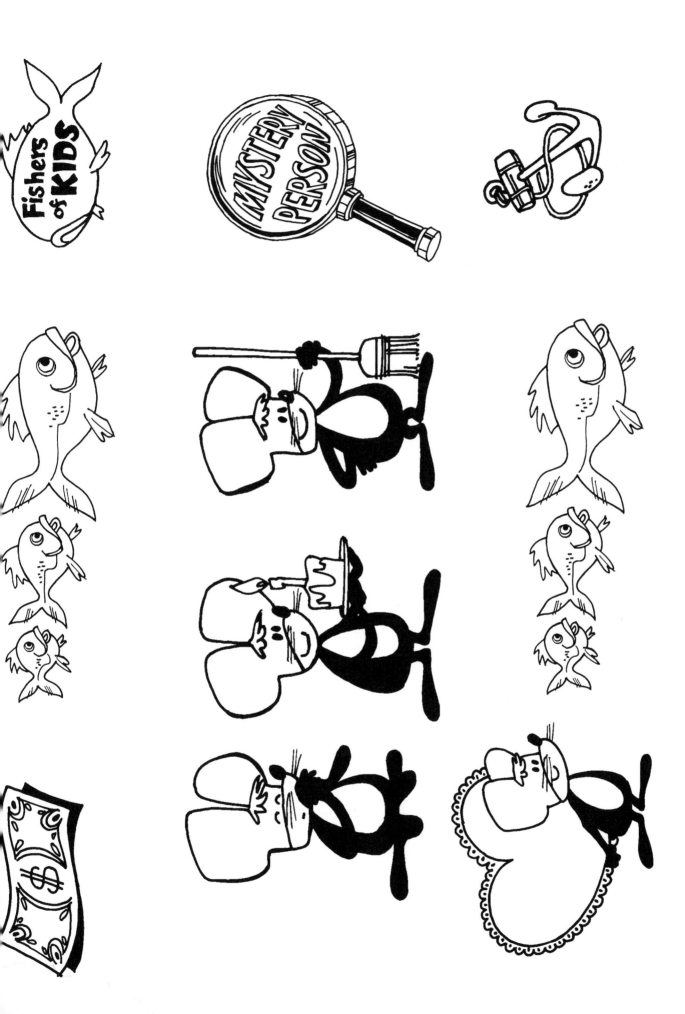

These pages include ideas to use occasionally in your bulletins.

Once you see how ideas can be used, let your creative juices flow. Design some of your own patterns on a plastic milk jug with a black felt tip pen and cut out. This can be a template for future bulletins—flat and easy to store.

Study and use visual words. For example, when you use words that pertain to heaven or clouds, pull cotton balls loosely apart and glue to the bulletin.

Specialized Bulletins

You can adapt bulletins to follow a special holiday or seasonal theme. Also, birthdays and helpers can be added to your particular bulletin. Here's one example I used.

Sample:

MICHIGAN is a great place to live, and here is a Michigander who is celebrating her birthday on the 21st.
CARYN WIERS
Another birthday will be celebrated a long way from Michigan . . . little ABBY SMITH has a special day in HAITI on the 18th.

MICHIGAN WEEK BULLETIN helpers are: Jason Scholten, John Jay Scholten and Shanna Scholten! Next week will be Amanda and Joshua Nykamp, Mike Daling and Shelly Daling.

—Mom charts the day
—Chalk one for Dad
—One of two children
—A quiet family member
—Handles notes beautifully

Who is this week's mystery MICHIGANDER? Mystery person blanks are by Skeeter's basket, only one guess each. Give a token gift to the one who wins.

The mystery character from the Bible last week—lives alone, has parents, brothers, sisters and keeps secrets—R A H A B! (use with Joshua.)

Vacation Bulletin

A special church family bulletin idea good for summer vacation time is to make a list of the last names in your congregation (use your church directory), then go through a U.S. atlas, scanning each state for these names and see how many members' names are on the map.
Example:

CARTER, Oklahoma
MCMURRAY, Pennsylvania
PIERCE, Nebraska

Include a 4" x 8" blank U.S. map in the bulletin. It should have states outlined but nothing else. Most school teachers will gladly make a copy for you. List the family names and states and ask children to draw a star at the state where the family name is.

You can also check over your own state and perhaps find enough towns with church families' names. In this case use only the shape of your state and enlarge it. Put circles in the approximate location of each town and have children put numbers in the circles to match numbers of the place of the family name.

Using New and Old Envelopes

- white is good
- colored is better

Pointed Pockets

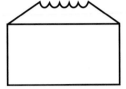

Cut a 1" strip from the bottom of the length of the envelope. Open the strip, lay the piece down and flatten. Then press down the corners. You can fold over one end making a pointed pocket for little notes or tiny flowers. Use as a bookmark.

Umbrella Envelope

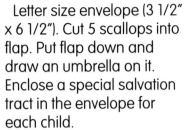

Letter size envelope (3 1/2" x 6 1/2"). Cut 5 scallops into flap. Put flap down and draw an umbrella on it. Enclose a special salvation tract in the envelope for each child.

Envelope Animal

Can you imagine an envelope animal? Just draw a figure from top to bottom, side to side. Cut all around the sides and bottom of the envelope. Leave the top as a fold. Open and spread apart and the animal stands.

Many of the items you will need for children's bulletins can be donated by people in the congregation. Publish a list. You'll be surprised by what people have on hand. At some places of employment items that would be thrown away can be salvaged.

Tools and Materials for Working and Assembling Children's Bulletins

- "dryline" by Liquid Paper
- "Handy Tacker" and whiteout for errors
- X-Acto knife
- metal ruler with cork backing (markers will not smear and cutting is easier)
- inexpensive round plastic toothbrush holder to store X-Acto knife safely (Put a cotton ball in each end.)
- varied size ink markers for additions
- supply of pencils and a sharpener
- scrap paper to work out patterns and ideas (junk mail that has a clean side for cut-out work, learning to fold, etc.)
- supply of paper clips
- small cardboard boxes, 12" wide to 6" deep to 7" high, for quick starter files. (I found Whitman candy boxes ideal. Check grocery and pharmacy stores for these.)
- rubber eraser
- pair of scissors
- easy to use glue
- paper punch

Check around the house for these things. A plastic case is great to keep all these things together as your personal children's bulletin tool kit.

Clip Art

Set up your own mini-file for small pieces of clip art that you may want to use in your bulletin. Next time you buy a box of 3-1/2" x 6-1/2" envelopes, save the box to use as a file box. Also save junk mail or letter envelopes that size. Tuck in the flap and print what the envelope contains in the middle of the flap. Sort your pieces, then categorize and alphabetize your envelopes by subject matter. This file will be at your fingertips: no more small art pieces wrinkled or lost.

Newspapers, adult bulletins, and junk mail have many interesting clip art pictures. Clip and file them! Some may be copywrited; keep those for idea-starters.

New and Ready-to-Go Stuff

1. Band-aids: buy plain, colored, or prints
2. Cotton balls: excellent for clouds and heavenly accents
3. Fish crackers: for N.T. stories
4. Candy: buy seasonal candy after holidays and store in a cool, dry place. Life Savers make good wheels. With a clean water color brush, wet one side of the Life Saver and place it where you want to use it. Let set and dry. It will be edible. **Do not try on a damp day.**
5. Sticks of sugarless gum, "Extra" brand
6. Color-coated paper clips
7. Two-pronged paper fasteners
8. Sponges: can look like cheese for mouse trap poem
9. Stickers and stars: add color and dimension to bulletin
10. Velcro: can be used to fasten special features to the bulletin. (Example: Christ's Ascension from the Cut-out section.)
11. Metallic pens, gold or silver: can be used to highlight words, add hand-drawn stars, light rays, lights in windows, or candle flames
12. U.S. flags on toothpicks, hearts on toothpicks, or sword toothpicks for Eph. 6 (Armor of God) (After holidays buy less than 1/2 price.)

13. Envelopes: some card shops have extra ones that they bundle up and sell for a reasonable price.
14. 2" x 3-1/2" reclosable bags (Check local mail and packaging stores.)

Macaroni

Macaroni can be a really fun thing in bulletins. Besides the alphabet macaroni, there are new fun shapes like bears, dinosaurs, umbrellas, and even musical instruments.

To organize alphabet macaroni, save two cardboard egg cartons for one pound of macaroni, cutting off the top and saving only the bottom of the cartons. Mark each cavity for each letter, putting "P" and "Q" together, and "X", "Y," and "Z" in one cavity. Sort 1/2 or 1 cup of macaroni at a time by pouring on a piece of paper. Store your macaroni by stacking the egg cartons.

An alternate idea is to use small plastic containers like Tic Tac boxes. Contents will be visible, plus the size and shape are easy to store. Mark an alphabet letter or a number on top of each container. Carefully spoon letters to Tic Tac container, snap and store.

Added Hints: Use little dabs of glue when you use macaroni and let dry before handling. With colored marker, go over letters or shapes. They will stand out!

S. O. S. (Save Other Stuff)

Many of the items needed to add spark to bulletins can be donated by members of the congregation. Publish a list and provide a collection spot. Then watch the donations pile up. Some businesses or organizations are willing to donate items that might otherwise be thrown out.

1. Colored envelopes: new if possible but old are okay. (Ask friends and relatives to save leftover odd-sized, envelopes.)

2. "Free-bies"—plastic paper clips, pencils, bookmarks, wrapped candy or nuts, bottle caps
3. Fabric scraps
4. Plastic hooks from new socks and gloves, etc.
5. Old house and car keys: for a "keys of the Kingdom" bulletin (disinfect and wash them)
6. Lace, ric-rac, ribbon, trim
7. Plastic milk jug rings: slip jug ring around rolled up bulletin
8. Milk jug patterns: fasten or clip on the bulletin (for some ideas, look in the Ideas section)
9. Plastic mesh bags: for fish nets
10. Plastic white foam padding: cut snowmen, clouds, etc.
11. Old stamps: for N.T. letters
12. Tags from bread wrappers: use tags with ribbons to make a cross book mark
13. Tic Tac or other small, clear containers
14. Velcro scraps: to hold special cut-out inserts
15. Wallpaper: to clip on bulletin; to make patterns
16. Yarn

Next time you buy a pair of shoes, ask for a box or two for storing your things. Affix a piece of masking tape on the lower part of the box and write on it what the box contains. These boxes don't take up much space and are handy storage units!

Children's lapboards

Check in your congregation for what may be available to make lapboards for the children. A man in my congregation was able to get small pieces of masonite, out of which my son and I made lapboards for children to use in church. The boards were cut to 7" x 10". A plastic tote was purchased (available in most housewares departments) to store the boards. The tote was placed on a table in the narthex of the church. These boards are used instead of the

pew Bible or the pew hymnbook to write on. The children and their parents are encouraged to use the lapboards to protect the these booksfrom pencil and pen marks. There is a simple tract available for teaching children how to handle and care for pew Bibles and hymnbooks. Send a stamped, self-addressed envelope to Natalie Moll, 11393 68th Ave., Allendale, MI 49401.

Books from Baker Book House

Children's Bulletin Idea Book by Faye
  Fredricks
101 Bible Activity Sheets by Betty De Vries
Bible Activity Sheets for Special Days by Betty
  De Vries
Easy-To-Use Bible Activity Sheets by Nellie
  De Vries
Children's Bulletin Clip-Art Book by Virginia
  Lettinga

Children's Tract Sources

Request by title as a sample, along with a
price listing and any other free samples they
may offer.

American Tract Society
Box 462008
Garland, TX 75046-2008

Faith Prayer and Tract League
2627 Elmridge Dr. N.W.
Grand Rapids, MI 49504-1390

Good News Publishers
130 Crescent St. Ste. B
Wheaton, IL 60187-5883

Child Evangelism Fellowship, Inc.
P.O. Box 348
Warrenton, MO 63383-0348
Check your phone listing for a CEF Tell-a-
  Story in your area.

Concordia Publishing House
1-800-325-3040

Sower of Seed
Box 6217
Fort Worth, TX 76115
Request a sample "Bank Eternal" along with
price listing. This tract can be the insert for the
Piggy Bank bulletin in Cut-away section.

Other Resources

For "Gospel Dollar"
Dock Halley
1705 Barbara Ln.
Connersville, IN 47331

Oriental Trade Co.
1-800-228-2269
For novelty items, also check novelty items in
  your area.

Current, Inc.
1-800-525-7170
Request the religious or school catalog.

Viking Press
1-800-421-1222
Request "soft designs" and other new paper
  samples.

Should you have any questions or difficulties
in assembling any bulletins in this book,
please write to me. I'll be happy to hear from
you. However, if you would like a reply from
me, please enclose a self-addressed,
stamped envelope. Thank you.

                 sing
               n. N.W.
310 ChassMI 49321
Comstock P